2-21-08

To Iona !

Quiet Guys

CAN DO GREAT THINGS, TOO

QUIET *Guys*

CAN DO GREAT THINGS, TOO

A Black Accountant's Success Story

By Frank K. Ross

as told to Janis F. Kearney

FOREWORD BY RICHARD D. PARSONS
CHAIRMAN AND CEO OF TIME WARNER INC.

Writing Our World Press
Chicago

First Edition
Printed in the United States of America

10 09 08 07 06   6 5 4 3 2
Cover design and inside layout by Denise Borel Billups, Borel Graphics
Edited by Mellonee Carrigan Mayfield
Cover photo of the Ross boys in St. Kitts, before moving to the United States: (l to r) Winston, Willie, Frank and Clarence.

Library of Congress Control Number: 2006927746
ISBN: 0-9762058-2-3

www.writingourworldpress.com

The net proceeds from the sale of this book will be used to provide scholarships to minority accounting students.

To Cecelia, for her unending love and support

ACKNOWLEDGEMENTS

There were so many people who encouraged me through this process and advised me as I moved closer to the finish line. But, some people, in their own individual ways, made this book possible. Certainly, without my wonderful wife, Cecelia, neither this book nor my success in life would have been possible. My son, Michael, and my daughter, Michelle, were there cheering me toward the finish line and at the same time serving as another set of eyes through which I was able to see this book more clearly. I thank them also for reminding me of the episodes in our lives that meant so much to me.

To my brothers, William and Winston Ross, thank you for what you've been to me throughout my journey and what your stories added to this book. To my sister, Agnes Jeffrey, and my cousin, Eulalie Heyliger, thank you from the bottom of my heart for adding the colors and ambience of what it was like growing up in St. Kitts.

To my friends and colleagues—most of whom I worked with throughout my career and a few of whom helped shepherd me through those years—I cannot thank you enough for taking time out of your busy lives for interviews for this book. Your memories and insight contributed greatly to this task. Though you all know who you are, I want to publicly thank each of you here: Philip Worlitzer, Caspa Harris, Richard McKinless, Bennie Hadnott, Dan Robinson, Ron McGowan, Theresa Hammond, Susie Kay, Angela Avant, Tom Williams, Elaine Hart, Bill Morgan, Dave Fowler, George Miles, Milford McGuirt, Bernie Milano, Bonnie Cohen, Jack Miller, Clark Richey and the Rev. Dr. William M. White, Jr.

CONTENTS

CONTENTS

To the Man in the Arena

"It is not the critic who counts; not the man who points out how the strong man stumbled or where the doer of deeds could have done them better.

The credit belongs to the man who is actually in the arena; whose face is marred by dust and sweat and blood; who strives valiantly; who errs and comes short again and again; who knows the great enthusiasm, the great devotions, and spends himself in a worthy cause; who, at the best, knows the triumphs of high achievement; and who, at the worst, if he fails, at least fails while daring greatly so that his place shall never be with those cold and timid souls who know neither victory nor defeat."

Theodore Roosevelt
April 23, 1910

FOREWORD

RICHARD D. PARSONS
CHAIRMAN AND CEO OF TIME WARNER INC.

When he first set foot on American soil in 1951, Frank K. Ross was a wide-eyed 7-year-old, dazzled by his first airplane ride and the cars, lights and snow of New York. He didn't quite know what to make of it. It was certainly a strange new world, far different from the small towns and sugar fields of his native St. Kitts. But, armed with strong West Indian values, a loving mother and the support of his extended American family, Frank K. Ross transformed himself from an awe-struck child immigrant into a pioneer in the world of accounting, forging a successful career for himself and paving the way for countless others.

Quiet Guys Can Do Great Things, Too is a uniquely American story. It is a story as familiar as the multicolored faces of millions of immigrants who washed upon the shores of Ellis Island through the middle of the 20th century in search of a better life. It is a story of sacrifice, courage, perseverance and faith. It is the story of an America still struggling to live up to its promise. It is the story of one man who made that promise real, not only for himself, but also for thousands of others.

As a West Indian immigrant, Frank and his family took a giant leap of faith when they decided to make the journey to America. People of color have always had unique obstacles to overcome as they strove to make a way for themselves in this country. But, imagine a young Frank K. Ross, unfamiliar with either the white or black cultures of America in the 1950s, living in Yonkers plunged into the thick of the civil rights movement and trying to become one of the first African Americans to make it in the old boy world of corporate accounting.

Like so many immigrants before and after him, Frank K. Ross quickly learned that the reality and myth of life in America were often at odds, especially for people of color. But he saw that not as a barrier to his success, but as a challenge to be met and overcome with persistence and faith.

In 1966, Frank K. Ross became one of a handful of black accountants in America when he joined the firm of Peat Marwick, which later became KPMG. He was a founding member and past president of the National Association of Black Accountants. He has been a staunch advocate of equal opportunity and quality education. He has consistently taken time to mentor young people. And he is a visionary who has always understood that just getting in the door of corporate America is not enough. You have to make a difference once you get there and hold the door open for others to follow.

Every young, aspiring professional, whether an immigrant from another land or a native of this great country, should read *Quiet Guys Can Do Great Things, Too.* It is a fascinating coming-of-age story and a valuable road map for those seeking success, not only in public accounting and business, but also in life.

INTRODUCTION

During the last few years, I was constantly told I should write a book about my life experiences. People would say: ". . . in order to understand what you've accomplished, Frank, you had to walk in your shoes; but why not describe to others what it was like to walk in those shoes?"

To my astonishment, friends and colleagues were convinced I had accomplished enough during my career that I should share my experiences. Even family members, especially the young members of my family—nieces and nephews—urged me to write so they could learn more about their uncle.

I have always been a quiet person who tended to keep things inside more than most people. But I have learned from each experience and moved on, whether it was in my professional life or my personal life. Most often, others involved in these experiences never truly knew the impact, both positive and negative, that the experiences may have had on me. That was the way I wanted it and that was the way I liked to operate.

My life does include a long list of "firsts." However, I am always reminded of what John Thompson Jr.—former Georgetown University basketball coach—once said when asked about being the first black coach to win an NCAA basketball championship. He said the only reason he was first was that he was given the opportunity while others who might have been more qualified never had the chance.

To a great extent, many of my "firsts" in the corporate world could be attributed to the fact that so many other capable men and women hadn't been given an opportunity, yet. In spite of the reasons, however, the reality—my friends and family tell me—is that the lessons I learned during those years are lessons worth sharing.

My experiences as one of a handful of African Americans working in a majority white corporate accounting environment during the early 1960s and 1970s are now almost textbook cases. And, like the handful of African Americans before me and the countless others after me, racism was an inescapable fact in our personal and professional lives.

Whether we were African American accountants making partner at our firms or African American financial investors making it in the business world, there were so few of us around that rarely were there opportunities for us to pick up a telephone to discuss or validate our experiences.

Like others who were the "firsts" in their class, I was forced to rely on my own instincts. There were, oftentimes, quiet supporters in our corners—people in our organizations we never knew about—rooting for victory, wanting us to succeed as much as we wanted success for ourselves.

In the end, as I talk about my experiences and, yes, my successes and failures, it has been the look in the eyes of young students and professionals that helped me understand that a book may not be a bad idea—to validate what I and many of my colleagues know to be valuable experiences and lessons learned in the world of corporate America. The students' questions and their thirst for some blueprint for success against the endless obstacles awaiting them in the corporate world compelled me to move ahead on this project.

This book is really two stories in one. First, it's a collection of memories and shared accounts of my past that gives you a glimpse at the personal side of me and at the things in my life that made me who I am and gave me the foundation to successfully handle life's challenges. Secondly, it's an anthology of my life experiences, lessons I've learned that

I hope will be helpful to others, especially young men and women seeking success in the corporate world of accounting.

This book is also a good luck gesture for the young professionals who come after me. More specifically, it's for the many students and young professionals who come to corporate America with neither the pedigree nor relationships that others are often blessed with. It is my deep hope and prayer that they will grab hold of at least one experience from my 38-year career and more than 60 years of life experiences and use it to make their journey a little smoother and a lot more successful.

PART I

COMING TO AMERICA
(1 9 4 3 - 1 9 5 1)

1

ST. KITTS

I have always depended on the memories of others to help me understand my early life on the island of St. Kitts in the British West Indies. My memories are the memories of my older brothers, my aunts, uncles, cousins, and, of course, my sister, who I discovered only after moving to America.

It was January 1951 when I left St. Kitts and most of my childhood memories behind me. From the day I set foot in my new homeland, America, it was as if my memory box immediately began recording all things American and displacing—or maybe overriding—memories of my earliest childhood.

I was embarrassingly quiet during those early years when schoolmates pumped me for information—for some exotic memory of my old home. None of them could understand how I so easily repressed those memories. Later, I understood that they envisioned a postcard picture of lush landscapes, vivid colors, exotic birds and colorful dress—Americans' idea of a Caribbean paradise.

Since adulthood, I have returned to my native homeland a few times and from an adult's eyes seen remnants of what my young friends expected me to remember years ago—the breathtaking natural beauty of the island; the intoxicating scenery; the warm, clear blue waters; the delightful, tropical climates; white sandy beaches; and the lively culture that is now less authentically "island" than it was when I lived there as a child.

Was the ocean we crossed on the plane to America too wide to carry with me the memories of the only home I'd known—those rich sights and sounds of the island, the men, women and children who populated my childhood? Was it possibly a defense mechanism since childhood memories of St. Kitts often brought with them shadows of pain?

I still harbor ghosts of memories of my fatherless childhood that never left me. I remember Sunday afternoons in St. Kitts. I remember how my three brothers and I walked home barefoot in the early afternoon after attending Sunday school at the Methodist church in nearby Basseterre, the island's capital. My mother rarely accompanied us to Sunday school, though she made certain we attended.

I remember the scorching, dirt roads and how we took off our shoes both for comfort and to test our endurance on the sun-baked paths. We lived on the outskirts of town, and I can recall the happy freedom of those walks home on Sunday afternoons—a wonderful reprieve from our mother's restrictions. A time of freedom any child would cherish.

During the time between leaving our home and returning in time for lunch, we enjoyed simply being children. My brothers and my family tell me, however, that I was always too quiet, too serious, never one much for play.

We lived in a place called "Monkey Hill," named for the unusual green monkeys that inhabited the area. As far as I know, it's one of the few places where the green monkeys can be found. Green monkeys were brought to St. Kitts from Africa centuries ago by French settlers and now nearly outnumber the human population on the island. My brothers tell me that our father used to go hunting for the monkeys, which liked to raid the sugar cane fields. Sometimes the monkeys would become such a pest that the government would pay people to shoot them.

Our home sat near the tracks where trains carried tons of sugar cane from the white plantations to the factory. I imagine the endless sugar cane fields must have permeated all of my early childhood. The long rows of tall, green stalks were as familiar as the blue sky and the dirt roads in St. Kitts at the time. Now, I know that because of my father's role as an estate manager for the sugar cane planters, our livelihood depended completely on the sugar cane fields as long as my father lived.

The road that carried us to Sunday school ran from Monkey Hill to Basseterre. It was not uncommon for us to break off pieces of the white planters' sugar cane as we walked along that road to and from church, eating it freely without fear that God would punish us for so small a sin.

We were careful, though, not to let the sticky juice from the sugar cane soil our Sunday clothes, fearing punishment from our mother or recriminations from the church mothers. I cannot say for certain if the hard, green stalks of sugar cane were as sweet and refreshing as I remember. I haven't tasted sugar cane since coming to America, and I never knew where to get fresh sugar cane in Yonkers, New York, where I spent the rest of my childhood.

Most of my memories of St. Kitts come from others. Certainly, I have heard stories, and family members have shared memories of my father, Reginald Ross, who died at the age of 54 after a short illness when I was just 9 months old. Growing up, there were few things I treasured more than hearing those stories and the shared memories about the father I never knew.

From the stories, as a child I imagined that Reginald Ross was surely the tallest, smartest, most handsome and most benevolent man in all of St. Kitts—in the whole world, for that matter. I imagined that everyone loved my father, which made me miss him even more. Though I have heard many stories about him, as a child and now as an adult I have maintained that early vision of who and what he was.

My father was born in St. Kitts in 1890. Things were a lot different then. The community was thriving. Sugar cane was the main crop on the island, and cotton was a popular trade on the neighboring island of Nevis. Both crops would eventually become too expensive for the small islands to produce. It was a time when people got around on horseback or by horse and buggy. My Cousin Eulie describes it as a time "before all the cars came, taking up space and making noise the way they do today."

As the first son, my father carried his father's Christian name. He was the third child of 11 children—the last two were twins who died at birth. His five sisters and three brothers eventually moved to the United States. My father was the only one to remain in the Caribbean. He lived in Antigua for many years before returning to St. Kitts, where he met my mother, Ruby Swanston, who was 15 years his junior when they married. While Ruby was a quiet, reserved woman; her tall, handsome husband was a very sociable person—the life of every party.

Reginald Ross made what was considered a good living as manager of two large sugar cane plantations in Ponds Estate and Needs Must Estate. He was an estate manager most of his adult life, during the time when sugar was king. He observed sugar in all of its glory as well as its decline as a main crop in the British West Indies. While sugar production had sustained the small island of St. Kitts for more than 300 years, 2005 would mark the end to its reign.

The rising costs of producing sugar and falling revenues had left the state-owned sugar industry deep in debt and forced the government to shut it down—declaring that the 2005 harvest would be its last. At one time, nearly one-third of St. Kitts' arable land was devoted to sugar production, and sugar was the mainstay of the economy until the 1970s when tourism took over as the main moneymaker.

My father enjoyed horseback riding and likely witnessed the changeover to automobiles as a mode of transportation. He is portrayed by many who knew him as a benevolent estate manager with very strong management skills. He always helped his employees if they came to him in need, even loaning an inordinate amount of money to his poor charges. Yet, when my father died in 1944, the workers who owed him money were nowhere to be found. They, in effect, deserted my mother, who was then a young widow—at the age of 39—with four small boys to feed and care for and really needed the money owed to my father.

My mother was also born in St. Kitts. She was a public health nurse and midwife. She suspended her work outside the home, however, after she married my father to become a housewife and mother.

Rumor in the community was that my father's mother never wanted him to marry my mother because they were not of the same religious "class." My father's family was Anglican, which was considered the elite; and my mother's family was Methodist, which was not accepted by the Anglicans. The two factions conducted burials in separate sections of the cemetery.

My mother struggled after my father passed away. Even though he was very popular and well-liked by the Canadian company he worked for, the company forced my mother to move off its property soon after my father's death. She was given 30 days to vacate the premises. Fortunately, my father had left her a home when he died, and we were able to move into it.

My mother resumed her career as a public nurse; this time, her duties were greatly expanded. She was appointed district nurse for all of Monkey Hill. According to family members, my mother traveled around the area making her nursing rounds on a bicycle—often riding long distances through the day and sometimes into the night to care for the sick and to deliver babies in people's homes. Oftentimes, she would see patients in her own home. Emergency cases were sent by horse-drawn carriage to Cunningham Hospital a few miles away in Basseterre. Cunningham was the only hospital in St. Kitts.

My mother is believed to have delivered most of the babies born in the district during the time we lived there. For her work, she was paid a stipend by the government, and her patients paid her in vegetables.

My family's standard of living was slightly above average for the island, given my father's role as an overseer in the sugar industry and my mother's role as the government nurse. We lived in a cement block house, while the average home was built from wood. Still, there were no luxuries. We did not have running water or electricity. People in town had to go to a central place to get their water. Electricity was paid for by putting a penny into a conductor. Each time the electricity ran out, you had to put another penny into it.

I can recall one family story that survived the travel across the ocean unscathed. It was about our Christmas tree in St. Kitts. It was decorated with candles because we could not afford electricity. The tree caught fire and almost destroyed our home. I have heard this story so many times, I could probably tell it in my sleep.

While the incident must have been devastating for my mother and my family, I heard the story as a young American, when the memory of St. Kitts was already fading for me. It was because of that distance that the story was less real, more humorous. It was as if the story and the family might have been someone else's—a story about another time and place where electricity was a luxury, and candles were used to decorate a Christmas tree.

When I started school in America, another memory from St. Kitts returned. It was of my school, a one-room building attached to the Anglican Church. Children in all the different classes met in one large room. The grades were separated by the placement of the chairs in different sections of the room.

My brothers and my American relatives tell me that education was much valued in St. Kitts. They said people valued education the way they valued water and food, all necessities of life; unlike in America, where many people take learning for granted. That was just one of the many new things I would learn about my new home, America, and one I would be constantly reminded of as I all but closed the door on my old home, St. Kitts.

2

New York . . . Home

We arrived in the United States in the middle of winter in 1951. While traveling to America, a major snowstorm forced our plane to turn around and land in Puerto Rico. Our airline put us up in a hotel overnight, making our first trip one of the most memorable of my life.

We were four overexcited, stir-crazed island boys on our way to America, flying on an airplane for the first time and sleeping in a hotel with an elevator and bellboys! Flying was a lot different then. We had to keep chewing gum to keep from having terrible earaches.

We must have exasperated our poor mother, who was already nervous about coming to this new world and leaving behind the old world she loved. She must have felt overwhelmed by her restless boys who had no cares in the world and saw this very serious transformation as a new adventure.

For our young eyes, there were so many firsts, even before we set foot on U.S. soil. Excited and afraid of this new world at the same time, we clung to each other. We whispered about everything—the elevators that went up or down just by pushing a button; the shiny staircases; the men in costumes guarding the door, opening it as they smiled for people walking in or out of the hotel. As darkness fell, we pressed our noses to the window, peering at the endless lights and the buildings that seemed to touch the sky.

Early the next morning, my mother rushed us to get dressed, to gather our belongings and hurry downstairs to catch a cab back to the airport. We couldn't sit still! In St. Kitts, we had been told that the streets of America were paved with gold, and we believed this until we came to New York.

When the plane arrived at Idlewild Airport (now John F. Kennedy Airport), we saw the glistening, white snow even before we landed. This was the first time in our lives we had seen snow! As we shivered from the cold, our eyes soaked in this amazing new world.

There stood my great uncle, Henry Phipps, who we referred to as "Uncle," and his niece, Annette Swanston—my mother's sister—who we called "Auntie." Little did we know, the two of them would become our American guardians within a year of our arrival in America.

Uncle and Auntie were anxiously waiting at the airport along with my father's youngest sister, Aunt Florence; my mother's brother, Uncle Alton; and our cousins, who laughed at our "funny accents." What a relief to see their smiling faces and inviting arms! More importantly, they had brought warm winter coats, for we were still wearing the light summer clothing of our native island that never saw cold or snow. There we were, all four of us, dressed in identical winter coats! What a sight that must have been.

On our first day in America, what we saw was as far from our reality as leprechauns or fairy godmothers. It was the huge number of automobiles that captured our attention the most. There was nothing in our past to prepare us for a world filled with these moving machines that swarmed the highways. We had never seen so many cars! We wondered if people were driving all of them and where could they all be going? Although St. Kitts had automobiles, most people, including my mother, got around on bicycles or horses. Auntie told us her father was hit by one of the first cars on the island.

The second most fascinating new machine was the television set. We were completely flabbergasted by this small box with people inside! Uncle had a car and a television. We were convinced when we saw this that he and Auntie must be very rich!

One of the first things my oldest brother, William, who we called Willie, did after settling into our new home was to turn on the television set. He saw a locomotive engine come straight toward him! He ran through the house calling us and telling us to come watch the train moving inside the television! We were all disappointed when we arrived at the television set and saw that the train had already rolled away.

We were, quite frankly, obsessed with these machines with four wheels that carried people wherever they wanted to go. Uncle's new Oldsmobile sat parked most times on an incline in the driveway. His shiny, green car with leather upholstery seemed the most beautiful of all! We wondered whether it was as easy as it seemed for my uncle and the other Americans to control these machines.

It wasn't long before our curiosity got the best of us, and we got into some trouble with our uncle's car. One morning, we decided to test our own skills against those of the drivers we had seen on the roads. Willie took the wheel, and my other brothers, Clarence and Winston, controlled the brakes and the clutch. I am not sure which instrument I was in charge of, but I am sure I had one assigned to me.

We quickly learned that controlling the car wasn't as easy as it looked, but by then it was too late. Before we knew it, my uncle's car was sitting in the middle of the street. There we were, four young boys scared half out of our wits, valiantly trying to push the huge machine back up the hill before our uncle found out. We weren't successful, however, and our uncle's punishment was enough to convince us never to "drive" his car again.

Uncle had been an indentured servant in the West Indies as a boy and was sent to carpentry school in St. Kitts. As we were growing up, he always told us of the 20-mile-walk he had to make roundtrip going to school on Mondays and returning on Fridays. After completing carpentry school, he worked off his indentured servant status and moved to New York. Because of his training and experience, he became one of the first blacks accepted as a member of the carpenters union, the New York City District Council of Carpenters.

Uncle told us how he had worked on many of the largest buildings in New York during the 1930s and 1940s. He worked on what was then the world's tallest building—the Empire State Building in New York City—and the U.S. Naval Academy expansion in Annapolis, Maryland

Unfortunately, Uncle was hurt on his job in 1946. The injury would eventually debilitate him and end his vocation as a carpenter. According to Uncle, a jealous white co-worker intentionally dropped heavy lumber on him. The accident caused serious nerve damage to his arms and left him without full use of his hands, which would shake terribly whenever he tried to work. Uncle never returned to work after that. We didn't know it then, but my uncle's only income was his small disability pension.

Three years after his accident, however, Uncle would endure another heartbreak. His beloved wife Olga was diagnosed with breast cancer and passed away in 1949. Ironically, her death would open up an opportunity for my mother and her four sons to come to America.

After Olga died, Uncle finally granted my mother's wish to travel with all of her children to New York. Family members many times had offered to send for the two oldest boys, saying they could only afford to bring some of the boys to America and would have to leave the rest for later. But my mother wouldn't hear of splitting us up. She had steadfastly refused their offers—insisting that either all four of us come together or none of us could come.

Uncle was an extremely religious man. He carried his Bible with him wherever he went. Although neither he nor my aunt attended church regularly, they made sure my brothers and I attended church services most Sundays. Uncle and Auntie—our new parents in America—held on to their Episcopalian faith. But they allowed us to attend the Methodist church, Metropolitan A.M.E. Zion Church, just blocks from our home.

Most mornings, including when we went to church, my uncle required us to stand at his bedside before we washed up to recite a Bible verse he had directed us to memorize the night before. In addition, we had to memorize a daily biblical verse from the religious publication Daily Word. We were required to locate it in our own Bibles and then fervently recite it to our uncle first thing each morning.

Following our recitations, we had to stand another 15 minutes, or so it seemed, listening to Uncle's review and explanation of the verses we'd memorized. I think I tolerated this exercise a lot more than my brothers did, especially as we got older. Years later, when my uncle would become seriously ill, I would continued this practice, whether he asked me to or not, in hopes that this would somehow help him feel better.

While Auntie shared Uncle's religion, she had a more balanced and practical view. She was a tall, beautiful young woman in her late 30s when we first came to America. She had traveled from St. Kitts years earlier to live with Uncle and his wife in New York. Auntie worked as a seamstress, doing piecework for mostly Jewish businessmen who owned small clothing shops in downtown Yonkers.

She was proud of her work as a dressmaker and designer. She was also very active in the International Ladies' Garment Workers' Union (ILGWU) and for some time served as a shop steward. She made all of her own clothes and always received compliments on her stylish dress.

Like most people in our family, our aunt was very closed and secretive. We knew very little about her personal life, and she never shared anything she didn't think was absolutely necessary for us to know.

Auntie was an independent woman, especially for that era. She had a "can do" personality that she passed on to us—often telling us that we could do anything we set our minds to. She was very strong-willed if she thought there was an injustice. In eighth grade, when I ran into the problem of a white guidance counselor not wanting to send me to a predominantly white high school, my aunt didn't hesitate to take up for me. She went with me to school to confront the counselor.

Auntie had a domineering streak, but she also enjoyed having a good time. She loved music and played both the organ and the piano. She once told us about how she had stood in line with thousands of people at Rudy Valentino's funeral, waiting to pay respects at his casket. She never married, though she had many godchildren and stayed in touch with many friends. Relatives said she had lost her one true love in a car accident. After that, she vowed she would never marry.

Our new home was a typical black, middle-class household in Yonkers. Like most families who emigrated from the islands, ours was a structured household with clear delineations between adults and children. Auntie was a self-sufficient, independent woman, while Uncle was a strict traditionalist. Our home was autocratic in every way.

Shortly after our arrival, we quickly learned our restrictions and our responsibilities within the household. Each of us was assigned daily and weekly chores, and our aunt taught us how to wash and care for our own clothing.

My uncle's home was located on Hunt Avenue in Runyon Heights, a black neighborhood in Yonkers. It was a large, three-story home with over 10 rooms heated by a coal furnace. The house backed up to a large wooded area. One of our chores was hauling in baskets of coal from the storage area on the first floor of the house. Another chore was bringing in wood from out back. My uncle burned wood as much as possible to cut down on the cost of using coal during the winters. My brothers always complained that I wasn't required to bring in much wood. They all had big baskets, but I had only a small basket since I was the youngest.

Though I was only 7 when I moved from St. Kitts to New York, somehow I have retained those memories. Most are fond memories. Some are not.

Family and friends were an important part of our childhood. We were always excited when our relatives and friends visited us in Yonkers, usually on Sundays or holidays. The visits typically consisted of Uncle Alton and his family, who lived in the Bronx; or Aunt Florence and her children, who lived in Queens.

During their visits, our normally quiet house echoed with the musical, lilting West Indian accents that reminded me of a St. Kitts I hardly knew and the family life that we might have had there. We were ecstatic to have children our own age to play with. After the drawn-out greetings of our older relatives, we youngsters would head for the woods for endless play and exploration.

Holidays were always memorable times in our home. After opening our presents on Christmas morning, we would set out to visit relatives and friends in Manhattan and Queens. Most of our relatives visited us during the summer to get away from the heat in the city and so their children could play in Uncle's big yard.

There was something magical about walking to church on Sunday mornings in Yonkers. Like my St. Kitts experience, I greatly enjoyed the short walks to church with my brothers. We took advantage of those walks to talk freely, joke or razz each other.

Something I found enjoyable, but ironic, was that on many Sundays, rather than send us to church, my uncle and aunt would pack picnic baskets and blankets and set out in the car for Playland Amusement Park in Rye, New York, or to some beach in Connecticut. Even then, we couldn't escape Uncle's religion. When they chose to spend Sundays at the beach, we had church service at home before we left. During our home service, Auntie would play the piano or organ, and her music could be heard throughout our house and most likely in others' homes as well. Even though my brothers and I couldn't swim, our beach outings would turn into daylong excursions.

Our friends in Yonkers always found it strange that none of the Ross boys could swim. They didn't understand that we actually lived inland in St. Kitts, far away from the ocean which surrounded the island. The fact that we'd never learned to swim, however, would not only come back to haunt us one day, it would also nearly lead to tragedy.

I was about 8 years old when I nearly drowned at a public pool in Yonkers. My brothers and I had gone swimming at the only public pool where blacks were allowed to swim. As I sat on the sidelines, I noticed everyone was getting into the pool by walking down the steps and then swimming off. It looked so easy, I decided to try it. When I walked off the steps, to my surprise I sank to the bottom of the pool! I realized too late that this was the deep end. After going down a few times, a lifeguard finally pulled me to safety. Everyone was stunned that I had nearly drowned! I was pretty shaken by this incident. It could be one of the reasons why I would never learn to swim.

———◆———

3

ANOTHER SAD GOODBYE

The happiness and excitement I was experiencing in this new world was interspersed with sadness as well. Within a year of our arrival in Yonkers, another loss would bring me face to face with that part of me I'd left in St. Kitts. As a young boy, my days were centered on learning everything that was new in my life—our new neighborhood, our new school and our new extended family. I hadn't noticed that my mother didn't seem to be sharing as much in our excitement and happiness.

My aunt and uncle had noticed. My mother's health had continually deteriorated since coming to America. My aunt and uncle wisely took her to a doctor in hopes that the doctor could help her recover. After examining my mother, the doctor said her health would continue to decline as long as she stayed in this country, and he recommended she return to St. Kitts. He said that more than anything she was suffering from homesickness and needed her familiar environment.

We never learned what was wrong with our mother; and Auntie never talked to us about our mother's illness or whether our mother argued against the doctor's prescription or simply acquiesced without a fight. We couldn't understand any of this. Surely, it must have been very difficult for her to leave her young children behind after she had fought so hard to keep us all together—not coming to America until we were all able to travel together.

Without clear memories of all that transpired during that time, my intuition tells me that my mother's decision to leave us was the hardest thing she had ever done in her life. I can also imagine that something inside her must have died on that plane ride back to St. Kitts; and it was only hope in seeing us again and knowing we were well-cared-for that kept her going after that.

It was an enormously traumatic loss for me, as I'm sure it was for my three brothers, though we never talked about it. While I had no personal recollections of my father, I suspect that his death caused me to cling even more to my mother—and her to me. Her leaving meant that that bond had been broken.

During this upheaval in my childhood, there was a teacher to whom I had grown very close to at my school. I saw her as a substitute mother to some extent. To my surprise and dismay, she left the school during that same time, as well. I can still recall how that affected me. Even today, I can't think of my mother's return to St. Kitts without remembering my teacher's departure from my school around that time.

I am no psychiatrist or expert on human behavior, but I suspect that this second loss—my mother's return to St. Kitts—was too painful for me, and I repressed my emotions. I am sure this had a great deal to do with the shaping of my personality—described by some as having an uncanny ability to compartmentalize my emotions and my intellect. I suppose there is much truth in this. If so, it is also a form of defense mechanism in response to one of the saddest times in my young life.

My ability to shelter my emotions so methodically would turn out to be an asset to my career in public accounting years later. That early habit of burying my emotions to lessen the pain would allow me throughout my career to work through difficult problems and situations without the messiness of personal emotions.

The trauma of losing my mother, I think, later manifested itself in other ways. I became even more withdrawn, more introverted than I had been as a small child. But, I also became more focused on performing well, achieving, pleasing my new parents—maybe in hopes of never losing them.

After my mother left, I was inconsolable for many days. It was as if something told me I would never be able to exhibit such raw emotions again; that I should get it all out at one time. After the crying had stopped and my grieving period was over, I buried the pain somewhere deep inside me and promised myself never to allow that kind of hurt again. The loss still haunts me—making any loss of a loved one twice as painful as it might normally be.

We stayed in touch with my mother after she went back to St. Kitts through letters and her devoted niece, Eulie, who frequently checked on her. Returning to her home didn't heal my mother, not wholly, at least. Her health was never the same as it was before we all left the island in 1951. Auntie regularly sent my mother money to make sure she wasn't in need. When my mother's health turned for the worst, Auntie sent the money to Cousin Eulie and asked her to take care of my mother.

My mother's brother, Kenneth Swanston—a Methodist minister assigned to different churches throughout the islands—visited us regularly in Yonkers. Looking back now, I'm quite certain my mother badgered him to come and check on her sons. I would later realize that he was trying very hard to be a father figure to us.

My mother was able to move back into her old home in St. Kitts. Most importantly, she had Cousin Eulie, who used to baby-sit for us in St. Kitts while our mother worked as the public nurse and midwife for the district. Although she was only one year older than Willie, as a girl Eulie was given more responsibility. She often had to take care of Clarence, who was always sickly. Many nights when my mother traveled the area delivering babies, Eulie would stay with us. Though we were no longer there with our mother, we all knew she was in good hands with Cousin Eulie, a well-spoken woman with a crisp English accent. In time, Eulie would become the caretaker of her father and her sister as well as my mother, who would all become ill at the same time.

Auntie never allowed my brothers or me to forget that we had a mother who loved us but was unable to take care of us. She reminded us that she was "Auntie" and that our mother was in St. Kitts. I realize now how young Auntie had been when we first arrived in New York and how much she must have sacrificed to care for us and to keep her promise to our mother—to treat us like her own—after our mother left us in America.

Auntie made us write to our mother regularly. But as we grew older, our letters became more of a routine. By the time I was in high school, I seldom wrote letters to her, but I sent birthday and Christmas cards each year. In all those years, my mother never stopped writing us and never once forgot any of our birthdays. One regret I carry with me to this day is that I didn't think to save my mother's letters or birthday cards.

In 1978, Cousin Eulie called to tell us that my mother had a heart attack. For the first time in over 25 years, I knew this was the time I had to go home, but I was afraid to make the trip. Unlike my brothers, I hadn't visited my mother or St. Kitts since we'd left in 1951 when I was just a small boy. The truth is, I had no real plans of returning there. I could never explain this unspoken decision to anyone who asked.

The only rational way I can describe my fear of returning home was the fear of facing my mother or having my complex emotions take over while I was there. I simply didn't know how I would react to seeing her. I had pushed my past and the hurt from her leaving so far back in my psyche that I was afraid to pull it out again. I didn't feel prepared to face any of it.

While I knew on an intellectual level that I had to return to St. Kitts, I searched for rational reasons not to go. When I accepted that there was no valid reason, I solicited my brother, Clarence, to travel with me. I could not do it alone. So a few months after learning of my mother's heart attack, I finally returned to St. Kitts.

In spite of the fear and anxiety that consumed me throughout the flight to St. Kitts, as soon as I arrived at my mother's home I knew I had made the right decision. Frankly, it was probably the wisest decision I'd make in my lifetime.

The visit to St. Kitts was not only a very emotional experience— seeing my mother for the first time since she left us—but also a surprisingly exciting one. It was as if I was seeing so much for the first time. There were people I met and places I visited that I sensed knowing and experiencing before . . . in another lifetime, maybe. And, in a way, that is exactly what it was—another lifetime. It was a strange, out-of-body kind of feeling, walking into the home where I was born; visiting the church where I was baptized as well as attended as a child; meeting family members I didn't recall but in whom I detected the Ross resemblances.

Family and friends on the island all came by to see Reginald and Ruby's youngest son, now all grown up and working in New York. They were well aware that I had not been back to see my mother in all those years. They stared at Clarence and me. I knew they were seeing our parents in our faces or our demeanor.

I remember looking at the small house where my mother lived and realizing how fortunate I was to have grown up in America. Although this house was considered one of the better houses on the island, it was nothing more than one or two rooms with a small bathroom. I also realized how lucky I was to be able to take advantage of so many opportunities in America that would never have been available to me if I had grown up in St. Kitts.

I would question myself during the flight back to New York, however, and admit that part of my hesitation in returning to St. Kitts was guilt for not visiting my mother sooner; for not being the good son she had deserved. I also wondered if my absence over the years was a result of my feeling abandoned by her. Did I stay away out of anger and continued to do so over the years to unconsciously punish my mother for leaving me and my brothers?

My mother passed away a few months after my visit. Cousin Eulie was a godsend in helping with the arrangements for our mother's funeral services, which were held at the Methodist church she attended. My brothers and I all returned to St. Kitts for the funeral—my second trip back to St. Kitts in one year. Uncle Kenneth officiated. It was well-attended, which made me feel good knowing that after all these years she was still well-thought-of by so many people.

There was an almost comical mix-up at the funeral, however, that only Cousin Eulie noticed. My mother's body originally was taken to the Methodist part of the cemetery because she was Methodist. However, my father was Anglican and was buried in the Anglican section of the cemetery. But my mother, who converted to Anglicanism when she married my father, had reverted back to her parents' religion, Methodism, after his death. So her body had to be moved from the Methodist section and taken to the Anglican section for burial beside my father.

Normally, the graveside services always took place in the evening after the sun went down. But because I had to fly back to New York that evening, everything had been moved to the middle of the day. As it turned out, because of the mix-up at the cemetery, my mother had to be buried in the evening as the sun was setting.

I left St. Kitts after my mother's funeral extremely happy that I had finally come home but disappointed that I hadn't come sooner. I had thousands of "what ifs" and other questions floating around in my head after that visit. I tried to imagine what it would've been like to see my mother in better health and at a time when we could've gotten to know each other as two adults—a time when I could have asked all the questions I'd buried away about her, about my father and about her leaving my brothers and me in New York.

I wished I could've had time to tell her who I'd turned out to be; to assure her that she had done the best she could and had left us with guardians who also did the best they could. I knew she would have been proud of me, if only I'd let her know.

Just before my flight back to New York, Cousin Eulie told me that my mother died peacefully, that she had held on long enough to see her "baby," and that she was satisfied once she knew I had turned out fine.

———◆———

Part II

My Life in Yonkers
(1951 - 1966)

4

GROWING UP IN YONKERS

My memory of growing up in Yonkers is that of an ongoing adventure, though most people remember me as being so quiet and unexpressive that they rarely knew what I was feeling. I was often told that I was too young to be so serious; that I should smile more. For me, every day was full of new and exciting happenings. I would wake up excited about what new thing could possibly happen in my day.

You have to understand the city of Yonkers in order to understand what it was like to grow up there and to go to school there during the 1950s. Yonkers borders the north of New York City. By the time we set foot on its soil, Yonkers was the fifth largest city in the state of New York.

From everything we had heard, New York was a northern state, which meant it was far more racially liberal than the southern states. That might have been true for parts of New York, but it didn't hold true for the place we would call home. Later, I would learn that it wasn't the whole truth when it came to any of the northern states.

Yonkers was a very conservative city, made up of mostly working class white immigrants who, like us, came to America to find their own piece of gold. They, of course, were not at all interested in sharing what they found with blacks, whether they were American-born or immigrants.

During my childhood, the two largest employers in Yonkers were Otis Elevator Co. and Alexander Carpet Co. The carpet company closed its plant while I was in high school and moved its operations to the South, leaving thousands of people unemployed.

The fact that Yonkers was a northern city didn't transfer to the citizens' attitudes about blacks—or anyone different from themselves. As far as they were concerned, integration was something the government was trying to shove down their throats. It seemed that the city's white leaders spent an amazing amount of time finding loopholes to get outside the federal decisions.

There was a definite line between the all-white community of Homefield and the all-black neighborhood of Runyon Heights, where we grew up. The housing patterns transferred over to the city's school system as well. Even though I had white friends from junior high through high school, that didn't change the fact that segregation was real in Yonkers. It permeated every aspect of our lives. Golf courses, recreational facilities, public schools and churches were all segregated. Racism was subtle, but as real as the "Coloreds" or "Whites Only" signs in America's southern cities.

Runyon Heights originally was called Nepperhand to coincide with the name given to its train station; but when the station closed, the neighborhood wanted its own name, thus the name Runyon Heights. Our homes were bordered on three sides by railroad tracks and major roadways. All roads leading into our community from the main roadway—Tuckahoe Road—were dead ends. Our street, Hunt Avenue, as well as all other streets in Runyon Heights ended at the wooded land that separated us from the white community, Homefield, on the other side.

This wooded tract would eventually become the subject of a long legal battle that my brother, Winston, would become involved in during the early 1970s. Winston, who we all thought would become a lawyer, would instead turn out to be a civil rights activist and community leader.

Winston was elected president of Yonkers' National Association for the Advancement of Colored People (NAACP) during that time and held that position for many years. For part of those years, he continued to fight the city of Yonkers and its track of woods in the courts. That piece of land became a symbol of intentional, institutionalized segregation in both housing and education in Yonkers.

Runyon Heights had been founded and populated by working-class blacks from Harlem who bought the land and built houses there in the late 1930s and early 1940s. Uncle was a well-respected carpenter and one of the earliest residents to move from Harlem into the area.

Our three-story home was located almost at the end of Hunt Avenue. The first floor of the house, with separate entrances on the side, comprised the kitchen and an open coal storage space. The house reminded me of a much smaller version of an English mansion. Uncle and Auntie's bedrooms were on the second floor, as were the dining room, living room and sewing room. There was a large foyer where Auntie's piano and organ stood, as well as a front entrance to the second floor.

During my college years, I found that the best place to study at home was at the kitchen table on the first floor or on a couch in the foyer, which for many years had been off-limits to me and my brothers. There were three rooms on the third floor, which was also considered the attic. I still remember the stifling heat inside those rooms in the summertime and the chilliness in the wintertime. There was no air conditioning, and the rooms were poorly ventilated.

Two of the attic rooms were bedrooms. My three brothers and I slept two to a room. I shared a room with Winston, while Willie and Clarence shared the other room. The middle room, which had briefly been my mother's room, was always left vacant. After my mother left, Auntie decided not to change our rooms. But when Willie joined the Marine Corps, Clarence, Winston and I were finally able to each have our own room.

There was an impressive amount of land and woods around our home. My uncle used the land to raise a vegetable garden, and he built a shed to raise chickens. He sold fresh eggs and vegetables to our neighbors. Two chores I hated more than anything were cleaning the chicken shed and weeding the garden.

We were raised in a close-knit community made up of hard-working laborers—women cleaning white people's homes, factory workers, retired people. In our community, everyone knew everyone, and the adults always looked out for the children.

Our neighborhood church, Metropolitan A.M.E. Zion Church, played an important role in our education. Even though the schools didn't teach us black history, our church did. During our summer Vacation Bible School sessions, we learned a great deal of black history, including James Weldon Johnson's "Lift Every Voice and Sing," which came to be known as the black national anthem. This gave us a lot of self-pride.

Most social activities in the community revolved around our church or the Runyon Heights Community Association. As whites moved further out, leaving their churches vacant, black church leaders would attempt to purchase the buildings. They once made inroads into purchasing a vacant white Methodist church in the neighborhood, but the white church leaders refused to sell the building when they learned the buyers were black. The church ultimately became a supermarket.

Our neighborhood was not isolated from the problems of the day—drugs, crime, unwed motherhood, etc. When I was in high school, drug dealers hung out on a street corner near the high school. There were several people in our community whose lives were destroyed by drugs, including a neighborhood boy who was five years younger than me. He was found dead on the roof of a Harlem tenement building. He had died of a drug overdose.

I think my brothers and I were able to get around the problems because of the support and nurturing we received at home and from the church. This helped us envision our future in a positive and a spiritual manner. It also helped us deal with negative issues as we grew older. We learned that we could rise above them and not be defined by them.

5

MY YONKERS EDUCATION

The first school my brothers and I attended in Yonkers was School No. 1. Soon after coming to this country, our teachers discovered that we were quite advanced compared with the other students in our grade. I don't think we were so much brighter than the other students; we just had more intensive training than our new classmates. In addition, the new public school was not very challenging for the students who attended.

Most of the teachers were new and young. Others, we'd learn later, were sent to School No. 1 as a last reprieve. The school system considered them low-performance teachers. To us, that tactic revealed more about the administration's expectations for the students at School No. 1 than it did about their actual abilities.

It was a very small school population. Only students from Runyon Heights attended School No. 1. A few neighbors sent their children to the nearby parochial school. When Winston and Clarence graduated from the sixth grade, there were a total of six pupils in their graduation class. My classes generally consisted of about 10 students.

School No. 1 closed in 1954. I had just been promoted to fifth grade. My new school was School No. 5, where classes went up to the eighth grade. We left home early each morning for our one-hour uphill trek to school. There was no bus service in our neighborhood. Moving from School No. 1 to School No. 5 also meant that instead of having 10 students in my class, I now had 25 classmates. I was coming from an all-black school to one that had only three or four black students in attendance.

In spite of the fact that blacks were a minority in School No. 5, I have wonderful memories of my time there. Surprisingly, the black students were well-received and made to feel welcome from day one, not only by the students but also by the parents and faculty. My guess now is that there was such a small number of us we didn't pose a threat to the rest of the students. I immediately found that the teachers at School No. 5 had high expectations for all the students and held me to the same standards they held all the other students.

When I turned 12, I was allowed to work as a newspaper boy, delivering the Herald Statesman newspaper in Runyon Heights. I worked my paper route for four years—from 1955 to 1959. The pay was terribly low, but I was just happy to be able to make my own money, most of which I made from tips.

In fifth-grade, I became obsessed with my school's motto. I walked past it every day hanging on the wall in the auditorium/gymnasium. It read: "Seek ye the highest." I can't say exactly why that quote stuck with me, but it did. From that point on, I made it my own personal motto. I consciously began demanding a lot of myself personally, not only from a religious viewpoint but also in everything I did.

There was only one other black in my sixth-grade class. There were about six in my eighth-grade class. We all lived in Runyon Heights and attended the same church. Many of the whites I befriended at School No. 5 remained my friends throughout high school. This didn't mean racism had disappeared. In fact, many white students at school disparagingly called our neighborhood "Little Africa."

One of my first inductions into the reality of being black in Yonkers took place during my transition from junior high school to high school. I had made up my mind that I would go to Roosevelt High School, the academic high school for students in our neighborhood.

Traditionally, most black students in our neighborhood were sent to Saunders High School, the local trade and technical high school, and encouraged to study for a career in trade. Many were sent to Commerce High School to study commercial courses. If a black student was lucky enough to go to Roosevelt, they usually went as a general student and not as part of the college preparatory program. The white teachers and counselor at School No. 5 would only recommend a few black students to participate in the academic program, and they had to be the best and the brightest in their class. In short, they almost had to have the IQ of a genius.

I desperately wanted to go to Roosevelt High. There was a certain status attached to students who attended Roosevelt, and I knew that going there would give me an edge in going on to college. In addition, all of my white friends were going to Roosevelt. When the discussion came up about where we would go to high school, of course, I said I would go to Roosevelt, too. We agreed we would all go to college. I had a problem, however, that none of my white friends had. The white guidance counselor wanted to steer me to Saunders to take up a trade such as carpentry.

Carpentry! I had no interest in or predilection to carpentry. I admitted to the counselor that I hadn't even been able to build a square box in my shop class. Once she conceded my deficiencies in shop, she began a new push for me to attend Commerce High School. Her first choice of major for me was cooking. Cooking? I have never been good at cooking, and to this day I hate cooking. Of course, my aunt and uncle never thought a boy should go to school to become a cook.

This counselor had also been the guidance counselor for my three brothers, who attended Longfellow Junior High School. She had been successful in directing my brothers—all exceptional students—to either Saunders or Commerce, where she regularly directed black students. Nothing my brothers told her had changed her mind. I don't think, though, she realized how determined I was about going to Roosevelt High.

When I went home and told my aunt what was happening, she went to the school to meet with the counselor and made every plea possible in hopes of convincing her I belonged at Roosevelt. Unfortunately, Auntie had wasted her precious time.

In my last desperate effort, I removed all of my emotion out of the equation and thought more strategically. I was tall for my age and probably looked like a football player. So I went to the counselor's office and "confessed" to her that the real reason I wanted to go to Roosevelt was to play on their football team, which was one of the best teams in Yonkers.

With that, she let out a sigh of relief and asked me, "Well, why didn't you tell me that in the first place?" It was amazing to see that my ploy actually worked. The counselor's demeanor had completely changed. She became much more cordial toward me and immediately signed off on my attendance at Roosevelt. Even then, however, she never agreed for me to be in the academic program, which was where I knew I belonged and where all my friends were.

It was my good luck, though, that the counselor only had to sign off on my attending the school, not on which courses or how many I took. I immediately signed up for the same five major courses my friends were taking. As I knew would be the case, my full academic load left me absolutely no time to play football. Of course, I never went back to talk to the counselor about that, either.

Looking back now, given the racial environment of the time, it could have been that the counselor was sincerely concerned that I had a trade that would allow me to get a job when I graduated from high school. I'm sure she would never have conceived of someone like me being college material or having the desire or the means to go on to college. I guess she never considered that if I could go to college, I might be able to do something other than a trade.

Years later, Winston would lead the NAACP in a lawsuit that would document deliberate segregation at Roosevelt High School. The documentation would show that of the 300 students enrolled at Roosevelt at the time, only 10 were black.

When I began high school, I was trying to decide what career I wanted to choose for myself. I was leaning toward becoming an attorney. I remember always telling my neighbors when they asked what I wanted to do when I grew up that I wanted to be an attorney. They were always amazed and said I was too quiet and would not be a successful attorney. My response was that I wanted to be a corporate attorney. Although I didn't really know what that meant, I knew that it was not the Perry Mason type. But all that would change soon after I began college.

I enjoyed my high school experience at Roosevelt, for the most part. I worked after school, at first delivering newspapers for a few years. Then I began working at a ladies' specialty store—The Fashion Shop—on Main Street in downtown Yonkers.

I surprised everyone, including myself, when I joined the high school choir. What was even more surprising is how much I really enjoyed it. I'm convinced that seeing how much my aunt loved music and listening to her play music all those years finally rubbed off on me. From that point on, I became a huge collector and lover of music.

Another thing I discovered about myself while in high school was that I not only loved business but also had a natural ability for it. The Roosevelt High yearbook staff placed this caption under my senior yearbook picture: "Frank will make a benevolent business boss." I was surprised and pleased by this. It reminded me of how people described my father, and it showed that my friends recognized my love for business.

Although, I was in a college preparatory program, I took every opportunity to take business courses. I also had fun in honors history, competing with the girl we all admitted was the smartest in our class. I was always competitive, and it gave me great pleasure to compete with her on history exams and actually get the highest grade many times.

I had teachers who challenged me and at the same time allowed me to challenge them. Because of that, my self-confidence blossomed.

My high school years paralleled one of the most important eras of American history, the civil rights movement. Though many people in our community failed to acknowledge it was happening, I couldn't ignore it. It was the height of the civil rights movement—an exciting time of sit-ins, marches and black power speeches.

My American history teacher didn't often agree with my position on civil rights, but she allowed me to do special assignments on the topic. I did a history project on a sermon by Dr. Martin Luther King Jr. about the injustice of laws. I argued the civil rights leader's position in which he said in the speech, "An unjust law is not a law." I could tell my instructor was bothered by my choice of subjects, but she was courteous enough to calmly voice her concerns. She lambasted Dr. King and his marches, but she challenged me to understand what Dr. King was actually saying and why he was saying it.

During this time of heightened awareness and discussion of racial injustices, I began to see racism in practically every facet of my life in Yonkers. I made a commitment to stand up against racism whenever I could, albeit, in my own way. I sought answers from my faith for some of the problems of racism and injustice. My questions likely convinced many adults that I was a good candidate to represent the youth of the church. During my senior year in high school, I was elected treasurer in the New York conference youth group of the Connectional A.M.E. Zion Church—a large international Methodist church denomination.

I enjoyed this time, primarily because it gave me an opportunity to get involved with other bright young people who had similar religious convictions and who were also active in their communities. We were all eager to make a difference. Most of us would ultimately become ministers, teachers, doctors, lawyers or other professionals.

I remained treasurer for three years. But I became less excited as the years went on primarily because our focus was so narrow. Our ideals of going into the community to help with the many issues of the day were not looked upon favorably by the adult leadership.

Like the rest of my life would prove, even my wonderful high school experiences were sometimes marred by reminders of the times and of who I was. Although I was still quiet, I was popular and had good friendships that would continue through college. Once people got to know me, they found I had a good sense of humor and that they could depend on me.

There was always that underlying knowledge, though, that no matter how bright I was academically, I was still viewed as different—less than my white friends—because of my color. I couldn't join my white friends at golf clubs, restaurants or recreational parks that many of them visited, and I was never invited to their parties or to their churches.

I still carry a painful memory of an incident that took place the summer before I started college. One of my white friends' father worked at a local factory as vice president of personnel. According to my friend, his father's company was eager to hire high school students during the summer, and all I needed to do was go to his father's office, fill out an application, and a summer job was almost a certainty.

I was so excited. I saw this as a godsend. I desperately needed money for my first year of college since my aunt and uncle had already told me they couldn't afford to pay my way. I was very eager as I hurried to my friend's father's office, confident that I'd be able to work through the summer and make enough money to enroll in college in the fall. Unfortunately, that was not the case. When I arrived at the office I could tell my friend's father was very uncomfortable. He finally told me he was sorry, but that I had missed the opportunity—all the positions had been filled a few days earlier.

I was deeply disappointed that day, but not half as much as I was later on when I learned that some of my white friends had gone to the office several days after I did to apply for a job and were hired right away.

That was a rude awakening for me, but I couldn't afford to spend too much time sulking over it. I let people in my community know that I needed work for the summer. Fortunately, a neighbor who worked at Otis Elevator helped me get a four-week summer job there and at a much higher pay than my friends' summer jobs. The job was hard factory work from 7 a.m. to 3 p.m. But it was great to be finished so early in the afternoon, and, most importantly, I was able to make enough money to pay for my fall tuition at Long Island University.

Despite constant reminders of the racial divide in Yonkers and in other places around the country, there were also some bright spots that always gave me hope. As it turned out, my new high school counselor at Roosevelt was wonderful. I had heard horror stories about high school counselors from some of my black friends.

I thanked my lucky stars that I didn't have to go through the same experience to get into college that I had gone through to get into Roosevelt. In fact, this young white counselor at Roosevelt went out of his way to assure that the few black seniors graduating from the school's academic program received the same college opportunities as white students.

He made sure we were given all the necessary information about colleges and scholarships and financial aid so we wouldn't miss out on possible educational opportunities. If we failed to sign up to meet with visiting college representatives or to complete our scholarship applications, he would remind us not to miss the deadlines. He also intervened with our teachers who excused us from class to meet college representatives. I give my counselor a great deal of credit for helping me get into the college of my choice and move into the career field that was a great match for me.

When I graduated from high school in 1962, my main focus was on going to college. I wasn't involved in civil rights activities like many people my age were. I didn't march for civil rights, nor was I a radical. But I have always harbored very strong feelings about any type of injustice, and naturally racism was at the top of that list. In my teen years, I became very active in the local NAACP and often voiced just how I felt about the injustice of America's laws.

6

THE ROSS BOYS OF YONKERS

When we were growing up in Yonkers, most people saw my three brothers and me as one unit. Our new parents demanded that we all stick together. None of us could go anywhere without the others. People began to refer to us as either "The Four Ross Boys" or "The Ross Brothers." They knew us apart, but were sometimes confused because they rarely saw us unless we were together. Even today, people refer to us this way.

While we were close, given our shared experiences, each of us had our own unique personality, and we liked it that way. If there was one Ross brother without a distinctive personality, I was the one. Given my extremely quiet disposition, most people couldn't figure out my personality.

But as much as we were different, we also had certain traits that must have been passed on from our parents and their parents and likely from the island culture we were born into. Even from childhood, we all shared a deep determination to achieve and a loyalty and love for family.

Auntie had taught us to be independent, to clean the house and even to wash our own clothes. All four of us worked from the time we were 12 years old—on golf courses, in bowling alleys, delivering newspapers, as stock boys in grocery stores or wherever we could land a job. We even did odd jobs for our neighbors—cutting grass, weeding, cleaning their houses.

It wasn't until I was 14 or 15 years old that Auntie told us we had an older sister who still lived in the Islands. Imagine what a shock that was to us! We had always considered ourselves a family of four close-knit boys. The news that there was a girl in our family was hard to comprehend. Our sister, Agnes Ross, was several years older. She was born before my father married my mother. She was, in fact, the daughter of his first wife's young cousin who they had adopted and raised. My father's first wife died after a short illness. This bit of family history was just as confusing to us as it was to the people we told it to.

We would actually meet Agnes in 1957 when she came to America with her husband, Fred, to go to graduate school. She was an attractive young woman and very nice. After our initial awkward greetings and introductions, we would become friends and eventually quite close. As strange as it had been to accept having an "outside" sister, I ended up accepting her wholeheartedly and being glad to claim her as our own.

Everyone always said that Agnes and I looked alike. As a matter of fact, Agnes had received a letter from our father shortly after I was born telling her that his new son looked just like her.

Because I was the youngest, my personality was likely shaped to some extent by my years of watching my older brothers. I was, to their chagrin, the one they were forced to "look after," to take along if they went to the movies or out to play. It was as if I was always catching up with them.

William was named for our maternal grandfather and carried our father's first name, Reginald, as his middle name. He was about 12 years old when we came to this country. Growing up, he always felt that as the oldest brother he had certain obligations—the British system required that the eldest boy in the family was next in line as the man of the house if the father died. And, even though none of us younger brothers agreed with this rule, William never let us forget his position.

William was the most outgoing—a natural people person, a true politician. He was always voicing his opinions and views to anyone who would listen. During his early years, our neighbors recognized his gift of gab, and most predicted he would become either an attorney or a politician. When William graduated from high school, he joined the Marine Corps and served five years.

After he returned home from the service, he enrolled at Pace College. William was bent on outdoing his youngest brother since I was about to graduate from college. He simply had to get his college degree, so he worked a full-time graveyard shift at a local factory, then rode the train to lower Manhattan each morning for classes. After college, he worked in adult education and later became a college administrator.

Clarence, my second oldest brother, was named after an uncle on my father's side. As a child he was the one who was most often sick. He was more technically oriented, sending away for models and building things as early as 11 years old. As he grew older, relatives and family friends would point out that Clarence looked most like my father. He was also the one that young ladies found most attractive.

Clarence's love for electronics was evident very early on. When he was in junior high school, he built a radio from scratch. We were amazed at his talent. Throughout his high school years, he entered several science fairs. Some of his teachers encouraged him to attend Saunders, given his technical skill. And, because it was during the pre-civil rights period, the school counselor encouraged him to take the "trade" courses, which would prepare him for an occupation as a mechanic.

One of Clarence's teachers recognized his talent and directed him toward the technical path—electrical engineering. He was very serious minded and early on in high school he focused on becoming an electrical engineer. This, of course, meant that he had to go to college, which was something I don't think my aunt or my uncle had given much thought to. I'm certain they expected each of us to follow our oldest brother's lead and enter the military after graduating from high school, then return to go on to college.

Thankfully, we were able to dispel that expectation right away. Clarence's high school teachers and counselor encouraged him to apply to Pratt Institute in Brooklyn. He was admitted to Pratt, but there was the question of how would he pay for his tuition? With the help of an ROTC scholarship and student loans, Clarence was able to enter school that fall. The hardest part was his commute from Yonkers to Brooklyn during his four years at Pratt.

Clarence was the first brother to leave home without going into the service. After graduating from Pratt, he moved to Cleveland and went to work for NASA's Mercury Project. He was, by far, the most brilliant out of the four of us; and even more independent than William. Given his focus on technology, Clarence found it difficult to communicate with us. He grew up pretty much a loner, coming to life only when he was forced to articulate his position on an issue he felt strongly about. He would never back down if it was a question of his beliefs.

Winston, the third Ross son, was born at the start of World War II. He was named after Winston Churchill but was given our uncle's middle name—Alton. Because of Clarence's propensity to be sick, he often missed school. As a result, he and Winston were placed in the same grade and graduated from elementary school, junior high school and high school together. Winston's counselor encouraged him to attend Commerce High School to prepare for a position as a salesclerk in the retail industry.

What people didn't realize was that we all had high expectations for ourselves, and there was also a matter of competition among the four of us. After Clarence was admitted to Pratt, Winston wouldn't sit still until he went, too—even though he had neither the college preparatory courses nor the money. To prepare himself, Winston attended New York City Community College and graduated in two years with almost a straight A average. He was then admitted to New York University and began to take business courses in retail distribution.

Winston surprised everyone, however, when he decided to go into the military after he graduated from NYU. He served two years in the Army and said it was the best two years of his life—it allowed him the opportunity to "see the world."

When he returned to New York, Winston went to work with the New York City Human Resources Administration as a caseworker. That initiated him into the world of social activism and community change. While working for the city of New York, he was offered a fellowship to complete his master's degree in social work from Columbia University. He also completed all the necessary course work for a PhD, but he never finished his thesis for his doctorate because he was "too busy" being a community activist.

Winston was our resident civil rights activist. He became active in the Yonkers branch of the NAACP and was ultimately elected as its president. During his presidency, the organization filed a lawsuit against the city of Yonkers, charging that its educational and housing practices together restricted integration in housing and the school system. Thus, the lawsuit argued, Yonkers was illegally promoting segregation throughout the city.

To this date, if you want Winston to become animated about a topic, all you need to do is begin a discussion about the NAACP or the Yonkers lawsuit. Although, he had been a quiet child, Winston was the typical textbook-case middle child—eager to please and satisfied with just getting along. It wasn't until he returned home from the Army that he transformed himself into a passionate civil rights activist.

The community of Yonkers and Westchester County and ultimately the state of New York sought Winston's counsel on civil and human rights issues. He became known as the quiet giant who was able to move mountains, influence politicians, businessmen and our city's political system.

Even with the competitiveness among us, my brothers and I were an extremely close family. We ranged from 15 to 17 months apart in age, and from the day we arrived in Yonkers, we depended on each other to validate who we were in this new world.

But tragedy would strike at the heart of our solid foundation in 1992, and we would no longer have the strength that seemed to come from being "The Four Ross Brothers." A stroke would claim the life of our brilliant brother Clarence at the early age of 52. His unexpected death was profoundly devastating to us. Not only was it sudden, but what also made it worse was that Clarence died at a time when he was very excited about his daughter's potential as a swimmer and about his son's upcoming graduation from high school and entrance into Morehouse College.

Upon hearing of my brother's stroke, I immediately flew to New York and had the opportunity to say my final goodbyes before he passed away.

During this period of loss, I received the following from a member of my church. This helped me deal with my brother's death in a way that I cannot describe but was very grateful to have received.

> "The pain is real. There is no such thing as pleasantness in someone's death. The one we love is gone, and the memory and experiences of life together remain. We weep as Jesus wept. We mourn. But the Apostle Paul tells us that we are not to mourn as those who have no hope. For in Christ, the hope of eternal life is a reality. We know that what Paul says is true, but there is sorrow in our heart. We know the promise, but we grieve at the loss."

7

A New Chapter in My Life

On more than one occasion in my life, I've looked back at some of my decisions and realized that without being 100 percent certain, I'd somehow made the wisest decision I could have made at the time. Some of those decisions were made on the wind of youthful arrogance, sheer naïveté and those blessings reserved for children and fools. Of course, there was also that mustard seed of faith that my mother, Auntie and Uncle planted so early in my life.

Beyond that, I have found that we immigrants hold onto something American natives often view as a Pollyanna attitude. Even as we strive to assimilate into the new, exciting American culture with its more cynical sense of fate, we remain convinced that fate is most usually tilted in our favor. Oftentimes, that means we keep moving forward against obstacles when more logical Americans might not. I am fortunate and grateful that this Pollyanna attitude has more often than not served me well.

A wonderful mentor would repeat that philosophy to me in much more eloquent words many years later, confirming my early beliefs. Of course, unlike me, this revered professional had already proven that he knew what he was talking about.

My decision to attend Long Island University was certainly one instance in which I made a wise choice without realizing it. I wouldn't fully understand that for years to come, but in many ways this small, predominantly white school was the site of my "rite of passage." I came into my own—found out who Frank Ross really was and what he had to offer the world.

A young man's cockiness some people saw in those early years or the "controlled arrogance" I was accused of in later years can all be accredited to my years at LIU. More specifically, it was during that "crossing over" period when I realized that I was bright enough to compete with some pretty smart students from backgrounds that made mine look a lot worse than it actually was.

But beyond that, LIU was the site of the beginning of a seam that would thread through the rest of my life. I met the most beautiful girl on the LIU campus, and she became the most exciting thing to happen to me during that time in my life. But . . . first things first.

Long Island University is located in downtown Brooklyn, right across the Brooklyn and Manhattan bridges. When I set foot on the campus as a student in September 1962, I was 18 years old. Demographically, LIU wasn't much different from the predominantly white high school I'd attended with just a handful of black students. LIU was much the same, except that the school of business where I ended up had even fewer black students. Like me, most of the students were commuters.

Temple University in Philadelphia and New York University were also college options available to me. Of course, realistically NYU and LIU were my only real choices. I couldn't afford to go to college away from home.

NYU had a much better reputation at the time, but I had what I considered practical reasons for choosing LIU over NYU. My brother, Winston, was already attending NYU and was also a business major. I couldn't imagine spending four years having to compete with my own brother in college or having to live up to his academic reputation if I happened to have the same professors.

There was a serious downside to choosing LIU, though. I had to commute almost three hours to the school and back home five days a week. That included my having to take two buses and two subway trains to get to school. I wasn't happy about this, but I accepted my fate and found myself a city map and a train and bus schedule to figure out my daily travel plans.

It wasn't until my first trip to school, however, that I got a real lesson in just how difficult this would really be for a first-year student taking 18 credit hours. Even though I took 18 credits, I had to take remedial English that semester. Fortunately, there was no school requirement that my grades remain at an A or B average that first semester. For the first time I experienced being a C+ student. In fact, I was fortunate to get passing grades in every class, except in accounting where I easily maintained an A.

After a semester of being in a funk about my grades, I finally figured out there was a method to the commuting madness. I could use all that traveling time to read, study and complete my homework. It was such a simple thing, but it made all the difference in my grades. It was one of those things I hadn't known to ask, and no one knew that I didn't know. Thanks to that simple adjustment, I would graduate four years later with a B+ average. Later during my career, I would actually miss the commuting hours I had used to read and catch up on my work.

When I began college, I knew I wanted to be successful—I just wasn't sure exactly where I'd find that success. The two careers at the top of my list were business and law. As a business student, I was required to take accounting courses my first semester and did really well in them. By the end of my first year, I pretty much knew in which direction my career was headed.

During my second year in college, I faced another personal loss with the passing of Uncle. He was in his 80s when he died. This was a very difficult time for me. I had decided not to work that summer in 1963 so I could attend summer school and have time to help take care of him. Although I had lived with him for 14 years by then, I didn't realize until that summer just how dogmatic my uncle's religious beliefs were.

I'm convinced that his life could have been prolonged had it not been for his idealistic religious beliefs. Uncle believed that God could do all things; that all things were possible; that all you have to do is believe. He put his life in God's hands and refused to see a doctor until just before his death. I tried, in vain, to convince him that his beliefs were illogical; that God works his miracles in many ways, including through doctors and other vehicles he makes available to us. I told him that having faith was not enough; that after asking God for help, we then had to take advantage of everything he made available to us to help ourselves.

Auntie tried to explain to me that Uncle was torn by his strong religious beliefs as well as the fact that his sick wife had gone to a hospital for treatment but never returned. He was afraid the same thing would happen to him if he went to the hospital.

Uncle's death angered me as much as it saddened me, even though I knew he had lived a good and long life. I learned a great deal from him and now know he did the best he knew how for us. I could never describe Uncle exactly as a father figure or my idea of what my father was like, but he was wise and innovative. He'd built his own home as well as two others on our block. He also built many things in our home from scratch and took care of whatever needed repairing around the house. He was a man ahead of his time.

For four years, I commuted from Yonkers to Brooklyn each day to attend college. I was so happy when I learned I had won a scholarship to attend graduate school.

It wasn't just the academics that heightened my sense of excitement during my LIU experience. From the time I was in the high school choir, I'd loved music and history. Imagine my excitement during my freshman year when LIU converted the Paramount Theatre building into its gymnasium, cafeteria and lecture halls.

The theater, famous during the 1950s and early 1960s for the Alan Freed rock 'n' roll shows, became a great setting for LIU's lecture hall. I'd walk into my English or history classes in awe of the knowledge that Chuck Berry, Elvis Presley or Little Richard once performed in those very rooms. That was exciting!

Although the university had several thousand students, the business school was small enough that I didn't feel lost in the shuffle or overwhelmed. The instructors emphasized the practical application of business, rather than theory. This was especially true for the accounting program, which was made up mostly of practicing certified public accountants (CPAs).

There were approximately 75 accounting students in my graduating class in 1966. It was a wonderful program that helped us develop confidence in ourselves as well as critical thinking and leadership skills. I knew most of my classmates very well and took many of my accounting and business classes with them. Nothing gave me better hands-on training than being elected president of the predominantly white Accounting Society of LIU and assuming leadership among a group of students who represented future managers, partners and even chairmen of accounting firms throughout the country.

One college experience I still remember quite clearly occurred during my freshman year. A couple of my white friends asked me to join their all-white fraternity. They let me know I would be their first black member. I'm sure they were sincere in their offer, and I should have been honored to be courted by their fraternity. In fact, I knew several of their members and felt comfortable with them.

I thought about the offer, thought it might be a great college experience and was actually flattered that they asked me to join. Beyond that, the opportunity to live in the fraternity house would also mean I wouldn't have to commute from Yonkers.

Yet, after giving it serious consideration, I decided it wasn't for me. I wasn't interested in being a trailblazer—not even to become a member of their distinguished fraternity. In the back of my mind, I imagined that being the first might also mean being the token black fraternity member. I wasn't sure this had anything to do with the offer, but I didn't want to take the chance. I thanked my friends, but I told them I would pass on the offer.

I learned later that the fraternity did recruit its first black member. He would subsequently become president of the senior class. I imagined there probably was some relationship between his membership in the fraternity and being elected senior class president. Even so, I maintained my position that the fraternity route wasn't the right one for me.

This was another instance when I depended on something someone must have instilled in me long ago to help me make the right decision. There are seldom any written instructions on how to handle certain situations. There are no "Do Not Enter" signs to direct you. What's more, many times there's no one who has had those experiences before. So you end up writing your own map as you go along. You have to know yourself and listen to that small voice inside you that tells you when something is right for you. Those voices, though, are sometimes terribly hard to hear, and you find that it is twice as important that you're a good listener, too.

My Uncle Kenneth, my mother's younger brother, would make an indelible impact on my life, which is why I'm so proud that both my son and I carry Kenneth as our middle names. What stands out in my memory about Uncle Kenneth is how he sacrificed each year, saving up his annual vacation to spend six months visiting us every five years in the States. I'm convinced that the main reason for those visits was to make sure that my brothers and I were OK. These were very special times for us.

During Uncle Kenneth's first visit, it was decided my mother would return to St. Kitts, and he was the one chosen to accompany her back. During his subsequent visits, he spent an inordinate amount of time with my brothers and me, and it wasn't until later that we decided that he hoped to fill the void left by my father and then my mother. I'm sure his own family wasn't happy about how much time he spent with us.

When I started college in New York City, Uncle Kenneth would often get up early to accompany me on my train rides into the city. He always left me in Mid-Manhattan as I continued on to Brooklyn. In the evenings, he would meet me at a designated Manhattan subway stop for our commute back to Runyon Heights.

During those times, Uncle Kenneth and I talked endlessly about topics I would never have been able to discuss with my uncle or aunt. I discovered that I enjoyed his company and our conversations. I would later realize just how meaningful that time spent with him was to me.

On one visit, Uncle Kenneth took me to the dentist after discovering that I had a mouthful of cavities and had never visited a dentist. We first went to a black dentist, but Uncle Kenneth became annoyed after the dentist started using Latin medical terms to explain his diagnosis. We ended up going to a white dentist who was very good and explained his diagnosis in simple terms. I would always remember my uncle's response to the black dentist and how he said it was never necessary to try to impress people with what you know. Years later, as a black professional, I always remembered this statement, especially when I was dealing with black clients or potential clients.

One of the things Uncle Kenneth always felt compelled to do was to remind my brothers and me that our mother's health was going downhill. He often asked me how I would feel if my mother died before I went back to see her, and he always suggested I do so before it was too late. He told me I might never be able to forgive myself if that happened. He desperately tried to convince me to return to St. Kitts to see my mother, just as everyone else did. Later, I realized that she had asked him to bring me home.

Thanks to Uncle Kenneth's constant yet gentle urgings, I finally got up the nerve to visit my mother shortly before she passed away. I would tell my uncle years later how grateful I was that he never let up. We remained close after my mother's death.

Emsar Bradford: A Real, Live Black CPA!

In 1963, during my sophomore year at Long Island University, Professor Owen Hague, a retired Army colonel, did an extraordinary thing. He gave me a full-time job while allowing me to attend college full time. I remember how excited I was when this opportunity came along.

Professor Hague was the only black accounting professor at LIU, where he was an adjunct professor. In 1963, he was the chief financial officer for the Bedford-Stuyvesant Youth in Action (BSYIA) program, a new anti-poverty program in Brooklyn and the largest such program in the state of New York.

BSYIA was created as part of President Lyndon B. Johnson's 1964 "War on Poverty" campaign. It would later become part of New York's Community Development Agency created in 1966—the year I left the program. The goal of the program was to provide services to the community while increasing the self-sufficiency of the people in the community.

In 1964, when the federal government sought models for the type of community involvement the Economic Opportunity Act addressed, New York City was already funding programs like Youth In Action in Bedford-Stuyvesant.

The Bedford-Stuyvesant area of Brooklyn was considered one of the worst urban ghettos in the state. It was made up mostly of very poor and greatly undereducated blacks. Bedford and Fulton streets symbolized inner-city crime.

In his first year at BSYIA, Professor Hague hired five black accounting students from both universities where he had taught—Long Island and St. Johns—to manage the bookkeeping operations for the projects. What an unexpected blessing for me—the opportunity to make money, gain invaluable experience and continue my education!

I was 19 years old at the time, and during the two years I worked with Professor Hague at BSYIA, I met a man named Emsar Bradford. What was most exciting about this encounter was that Emsar Bradford was the first real, live black CPA I had ever met! He was the 60th black CPA in the United States. I was always amazed to see him park his long, beautiful Cadillac right in front of our office. It was in one of the most crime-ridden areas of the city, yet no one would bother it all day. Emsar Bradford was such an impressive figure. We all loved it when he took time to come down and talk to us, mostly encouraging us to continue on our chosen paths.

His personal concern about our future left a lasting impression on me. When I talked to him about my interest in working in the accounting field, he talked about how difficult it had been for him and the handful of other black CPAs who got their licenses during the 1940s and 1950s.

Emsar Bradford had to move from New York to Maryland to gain his CPA license in 1960. Most states required that CPA candidates have apprenticeships or experience in an accounting firm before they were allowed to take the CPA exam. Candidates also had to submit a photograph of themselves. At a time when segregation was not only accepted but also legal, these stipulations all but cut blacks out of the accounting field. Moreover, few black accounting firms existed at that time, and no white firms would give black accountants the experience required to become a CPA. Even if they had, once the exam administrators received the black candidates' photos, they were pretty much locked out.

Ironically, it was Illinois, a Midwestern state—not New York or another northern state—that claimed the largest number of black CPAs. For several years, Illinois had no apprenticeship or photo requirements for candidates to take the CPA exam. Unfortunately, that would change over time.

Emsar Bradford remains on my short list of mentors who made a lasting impact on my life. Beyond all the intrinsic benefits of working at BSYIA, the material ones weren't so bad either. I purchased my first car— a 1957 Chevrolet Impala—thanks to my job with BSYIA.

I learned a lot about the cultural differences between blacks who lived in the ghetto areas of the city and those outside that area. Having grown up in Yonkers, I had not had much interaction with blacks from either inside the city or the area referred to as the ghetto. This was an interesting experience. Although I grew up in a black neighborhood and went to a black church, I had never really dealt with inner-city blacks. This job gave me my first experience working with inner-city blacks. I will admit that at first I was a little intimidated. But I soon learned that by treating them the same way I treated anyone else—with respect and honesty—they quickly returned the respect.

By 1966, when I was a senior and considering my options for my career, Emsar Bradford had become my role model. I already knew how much I could learn from him, and I was hopeful that he'd been impressed enough with my work to offer me a professional position with his firm. He didn't. And it was one of those mixed blessings that he didn't. He was wise enough to convince me to first test myself out at one of the big accounting firms. He was sure that was the route I should go. At first, I felt very disappointed, but later I realized why he did what he did.

Even after being hired by one of the largest accounting firms in the country—Peat, Marwick, Mitchell & Co.—I still had not gotten that vision of Emsar Bradford and my desire to follow in his footsteps out of my system.

Some of the country's most profound events took place during the years I was a student at Long Island University. The civil rights movement, which was evident even during my high school years, was in full swing throughout the country. President John F. Kennedy was assassinated during my sophomore year, and Lyndon B. Johnson (the genesis of the anti-poverty program I worked with) had taken his place.

LIU didn't have any formal black organizations on campus, but I recall that the campus closed for several days. A few professors held open discussions about the death of JFK in some classes when we returned to school.

I kept informed of the civil rights movement through television, newspapers and endless conversations with Winston, who never tired of talking about what changes needed to be made in the system and the blatant injustices being carried out. I have always been proud of the role my brother played in the civil rights effort.

I could see his passion for change as he delved deeper and deeper into the movement. Winston was sincere in his desire to work toward equality and justice for black Americans. Ironically, one of the first black CPAs in the country, Jesse B. Blayton, Sr., who taught at Atlanta University, became Dr. Martin Luther King's accountant after the state of Alabama charged the civil rights leader with tax evasion. Dr. King was later acquitted.

When people my age get together and begin discussing our lives, two key questions always come up. The first is what did we do during the civil rights movement? And the second is what was our military status during the Vietnam War?

When I graduated from college, I was elected treasurer of the Yonkers' branch of the NAACP. When people would ask me why I wasn't more radical or why I never participated in the civil rights marches, I would tell them how much I admired Dr. King and how the world needed people like him to do what he was doing. I explained that we also needed all the people who went out into the streets, fought, risked their lives and did sit-ins. Though I was not such an activist, I was no less committed to doing all in my power to make this a better world for all people.

I believed then, and I believe now, that everyone can contribute to help solve the world's problems in different ways. We cannot all be leaders or be out front in the fight, but we all can do something. I've always focused on the future and been willing to work as hard as possible to prepare, not just myself but anyone I could, for a successful future.

I believe people need to be prepared to move our race and our cause forward. Dr. King would not have been able to declare victories had there not been people prepared to walk into those doors he had fought to swing open. The same is true today. While I initially wanted to be a corporate attorney, I knew I wasn't qualified at the time and needed to prepare myself to be ready when the doors opened for us.

Years later when I became a partner at Peat Marwick, I couldn't be absolutely sure that part of the reason I was chosen didn't have to do with the company's need to add a black face to their partner roster that year. But that was more their problem than mine, for I would never allow my being black to serve as an excuse for not staying there.

I've never allowed my race to get in the way of what I wanted in my life, either. I worked hard to make sure I was as qualified as my white colleagues. I wasn't naïve enough to believe that most of the whites and some of the blacks with whom I worked probably assumed I arrived at that point in my career because of my color, but I always knew that, in the end, my work would decide how far I would go.

Toward the end of the 1960s, the nation was moving out of the civil rights era and focusing on the Viet Nam War. With the increasing buildup of U.S. troops in Viet Nam, I faced the question of whether I should join the military.

While I was in college, I had avoided the draft with a 2-S student deferment. But I knew I would lose this deferment upon graduation and most likely become a 1-A. Many people joined the National Guard or the Army Reserve to avoid active duty. I tried both but learned that I did not have the family connection to get my name moved up to the top of the list. My name was so far down that I knew I would never be able to join either branch of the military. I decided to continue my 2-S deferment by attending graduate school full time while working at Peat Marwick. This was not easy, but it allowed me to meet my future wife, Cecelia.

By the time I graduated from college in 1968 with my MBA, I was out of deferment opportunities. Even though I was married and had my first child, deferments were no longer granted. I went through the entire battery of pre-military tests and found myself classified 1-A. At that point, I decided to just wait to be drafted and hopefully based on my work experience and education I would be assigned to a desk job. However, I was never drafted. Although they did not have a formal deferment for married men with children, I guess they still put us last on the list. Also, as long as the Selective Service district you were in met its quota, you were not selected for the draft. I guess Yonkers always met its quota.

¶

PHILIP WORLITZER: A COLLEGE MENTOR

Philip Worlitzer, an accounting professor at LIU and chairman of the accounting department, was also an important mentor during my college years. The unusually kind professor taught most of my accounting courses. I got to know him, and maybe because of that, I was happy that I did exceptionally well in his classes. We often talked after or before classes, and the conversation would center on my course work but often expand to other things going on in the world. I learned a lot from those conversations.

I graduated from LIU with a bachelor's degree in accounting in 1966, just around the time the previously all-white accounting firms began opening their doors to a few black accounting graduates. As a result, out of the four Big Eight accounting firms I interviewed with, I received job offers from all four.

For whatever reason, I didn't tell my professors I had received these offers, though I had full intention of sharing my good news with Professor Worlitzer. I guess I didn't get around to it fast enough. As I walked from class with a friend near the end of our senior year, he told me Professor Worlitzer was concerned about my job prospects, and he suggested I find the time to go by and speak with the professor.

After talking with a few other classmates, it seemed to be common knowledge among my group of friends that Professor Worlitzer was concerned about my being picked up by a recruiter or a firm and whether I'd be able to get the required work experience needed to be a CPA.

By the time I went to his office to talk with him, Professor Worlitzer had already spoken with a friend of his and convinced him to hire me into his firm. Apologetically, I told him I had interviewed with four of the top eight accounting firms and been offered jobs by all four. I proudly told him I had accepted an offer from Peat Marwick. I couldn't be sure what Professor Worlitzer's true feelings were after that conversation.

Over the years I had the opportunity to visit LIU several times to speak with student groups, and every time Professor Worlitzer would show up to greet me. He is now probably in his 80s but still teaching a course every year.

Professor Worlitzer would sometimes embarrass me by calling me the "perfect student." During an interview in 2005, he reflected on the times he taught me as a young accounting student at LIU:

> *"Frank was the perfect student. He had the drive, the energy . . . and he must have had the discipline. The things that have helped him throughout his career were there then—that humility, that energy . . . and the focus. He was a very conservative young man, and all of his time and energy seemed to go to his classes. Unlike many students then and now, he wasn't the type to try to project himself onto you. He just soaked in all he could.*
>
> *"Every teacher wants to teach the good student. Frank was such a pleasure to teach that you found yourself trying to stuff every bit of knowledge into him you thought he might need. I've always tried to guide the students, and I got a kick out of having a young person around like Frank, who didn't really need much guidance. He was with us for four years.*
>
> *"I've kept up with Frank over the years, as I have with many of my students. One thing I remember is that he showed so much humility back then, I wasn't sure he'd have it in him to rise to the top like he did.*

"The essence of someone like Frank is that he personified the old adage: 'Treat your neighbor as you would have them treat you.' In spite of the fact that he was one of the founders of the National Association of Black Accountants, he never was a 'rabble-rouser.' He succeeded by showing through his success.

"Frank persevered by making NABA a real top-notch organization, and I can't really remember him ever raising his voice. Again, he showed by example that if young people use what they have—their brains—people will recognize that they have what it takes.

"Long Island University is far different from what it was when Frank was here. Black students are hardly a novelty anymore. And Frank has been very giving of his time and financial contributions. He comes back and talks to the students."

10

MEETING CECELIA

Beyond the fact that I found a comfortable niche for myself, made lifelong friends and became even more competitive during my years at LIU; one of the most important incidents to take place at the university was meeting my wife, Cecelia.

Because LIU was mostly a commuter school, the blacks on campus almost always hung out in the cafeteria between classes because we didn't have many other places to go. We also regularly sat at two specific tables. Many of the black students played cards to while away the time between classes.

People like me, who never really played cards, would stop by a few times during the day to eat, study or catch up with what was going on. It wasn't until my senior year that I began to notice this one very beautiful girl sitting in the cafeteria every time I came in. I'm sure she probably had been there throughout the school year, but I'd always been too focused on my books and preparation for tests to notice her.

Even after my first time seeing her, I was still too busy with my senior-year classes, my job and going to interviews to stop by and introduce myself or talk with her. The following year, after landing a job with Peat Marwick, I was still going to school, taking 12 credit hours toward my MBA. On Columbus Day—October 12, 1966—I was off work, but I went to LIU to study.

I spent most of the day in the library, but late in the afternoon I met a few friends and went to the cafeteria. We didn't go to the tables where the usual group hung out but sat separately at another table. Again, I saw this beautiful girl sitting there. This time I asked my friends if they knew her. One said he did and offered to introduce me.

He went over and tried to get her to come meet me, but she refused, saying she was in the middle of a card game. I guess this was the start of the inevitable. During the next few days as I went to my classes in the evening I would see her. I finally got up the courage to introduce myself.

Cecelia Mann was a beautiful, young woman with a quick wit and a charming personality. We eventually went on a date, and, as one would say, the rest is history. To this day I kid her by saying that while she was at LIU she majored in "cafeteriology."

Cecelia, naturally, remembers our meeting a little differently from the way I remember it. But whichever is closest to reality, the outcome is the same—I met the woman of my dreams, and she has been important to every aspect of my life since that meeting. We both agree that our meeting was fate, and I cannot imagine my life would have been half as wonderful if I had met another young woman in the university cafeteria that day.

Cecelia and I were married 14 months later—two days before Christmas in 1967. It was a nice wedding day, except for a few glitches. First, Cecelia was an hour late for the ceremony. The priests who counseled us kept assuring me that my future bride was too much in love with me to not show up. Later, I found out that she was waiting for her father, who went to help the catering truck after it broke down in the snow.

After the wedding, we planned a short honeymoon in the Poconos in Pennsylvania. Unfortunately, it was December in New York, and the streets were icy after a big snowstorm. Cecelia left to go home to change into traveling clothes, but she slipped on the pavement and tore some ligaments. We didn't cancel our honeymoon, however. My brother, Winston, and his then fiancée, Rosalind, took us to the drugstore to buy some Absorbine Jr. and Ben Gay pain relieving ointments for Cecelia.

The cottage we stayed in still had a strong scent of Ben Gay even as we checked out. I remember how strangely the housekeeper looked at us as we were leaving.

Poor Cecelia was still limping when we returned to New York. Our first stop was at a Christmas party at Auntie's house. I had to endure all kinds of jokes from the relatives. Yet, with all the drama in our lives at that time, we felt that we could still manage to laugh and have lots of fun together. This was one of the first indications of how our marriage would survive.

I think our families and friends were totally shocked that we would get married, or even that our marriage would last. We are such opposites at times and at other times we are in complete sync. We usually tell people that it is the craziness in life that keeps us laughing and makes our marriage work. We have a good foundation that was intrinsic in building a strong relationship.

While some people describe Cecelia as the wind beneath my wings, she sees herself more as my alter ego—expressing what I think and feel but doesn't always say. It's interesting seeing myself through Cecelia's eyes. Never one with a loss for words, this is what Cecelia had to say about me:

> *"The funny thing is people believe that because I speak out, I control Frank. Little do they know, I've always been in the background . . . not controlling him, but supporting him. No one controls Frank Ross, except Frank Ross.*
>
> *"Frank is such a giving person—giving back to the community, giving opportunities to young people. He has contributed so much over the years to the Urban League, the Iona Senior Services program . . . . It's amazing how he has gotten the most controlling and needy people that no one else can deal with to respect him.*

"If you work with him you learn quickly to respect him. He's a very honest person and never wanted to play games. He has a reputation for being a straight shooter. You won't find him on the golf course or at the Country Club, but more in your office meeting room . . . or helping some community-based organization. He never sought recognition for the many things he has accomplished in his life."

Out of our marriage came two wonderful children, Michelle and Michael. As I began to write this book, I wondered about what they really thought about their father. I knew I worked long hours and maybe did not spend as much quality time with them as they would have liked. So I asked Michelle for her opinion about me, and this is what she had to say:

"I believe I have a lot of my father's traits. While I'm not a workaholic like I used to think he was, I did learn from him that if I make a commitment I should do all I can to make sure I keep it.

"It's my father's philosophy that money doesn't bring you happiness.

"While people at my father's workplace always saw him as a mentor or a great leader, I never stopped seeing him as a supportive dad.

"One of my warmest childhood memories is how my friends mistook my father for Reggie Jackson one day when he came out and played baseball with us. As busy as he always was during our childhood, he always supported me and my brother when we played sports. My father was an avid baseball fan.

"He is the hardest working man I've ever met. But he also believes in giving back to his community and his family . . . that's a huge part of who he is. He gives out of joy and love, not out of a sense of obligation."

When I asked Michael—who, like his mother, is very opinionated—for his thoughts about me, this is how he summed me up as a father:

> *"My father is a hard-working, passionate man with a strong sense of fairness and strong commitments to his family and his work. He has a wry sense of humor that only he gets most times.*
>
> *"My perception of my father has changed as I've become an adult. Now, I realize how fair he was in his expectations and his parental disciplines.*
>
> *"I've grown to have even more respect for him, as I realize some of the things he must have gone through in the business world.*
>
> *"I believe my father's legacy will be that 20 to 30 years from now, people who have known him over the years will be able to see what amazing accomplishments he was able to make. And they will be in awe of how he was able to do it within the natural constraints of the times—able to maintain such a fine balance between his personal interests, charities, church and his business life . . . yet always have time for his family.*
>
> *"I believe that my father is considered a great leader because, first and foremost, people respect Frank Ross for his fairness, his heart and his integrity. If Frank Ross says he will do something, he will do it.*
>
> *"My father taught me values and life lessons more by example than sitting down and telling me right from wrong. Looking back, I can say his rules were fair. Just from watching him, I understood the importance of working hard and having a balance between our personal lives and our work."*

During the same year I began dating Cecelia, our dear Auntie came down with tubercular meningitis. Willie and I were still living at home then. In spite of our efforts, Auntie refused to go to the doctor. I had made up my mind that my uncle's fate would not become Auntie's, if I could help it. I made every effort to get her to see a doctor. After months of trying, I finally convinced her to go to the hospital. By that time, the disease had attacked her brain. She was forced to remain in the hospital to recover for a full year.

When Auntie returned home, she wasn't the same independent, strong-willed woman she'd been all through my childhood. The inability to recover fully brought with it a lot of frustration on her part. The illness changed her from a strong, beautiful woman of sharp intelligence and patience to someone who had little patience and was merely a shell of her old self. She could no longer work or drive a car. She now lacked the independence that was so important to her.

Though Cecelia's and my wedding day on December 23rd, 1967, was one of the happiest days of my life, the only sadness was that Auntie was not able to share it with us. Thankfully, the doctors allowed her to come home two days later on Christmas Day, and we were able to join her at home that night when we returned from our honeymoon and include her in our celebration. Because of my work commitment, Cecelia and I had only taken a couple of days for our honeymoon.

The Auntie that my children were able to meet some years later, unfortunately, wasn't the same Auntie I had known growing up. I regret that they didn't have the experience of knowing her at her best. We felt blessed, though, that she lived until the early 1980s. She was in her 70s at the time of her death.

PART IV

MY LIFE IN CORPORATE ACCOUNTING
(1966-2003)

11

My Entrée into Public Accounting

As a junior in college, I was responsible for arranging programs for the Accounting Society of LIU. Many of the programs involved inviting speakers from government; mostly the Internal Revenue Service, major corporations or the Big Eight accounting firms. I was able to get Coopers & Lybrand (now PricewaterhouseCoopers or PwC) and Peat Marwick to come to campus.

As a result of their campus visit, Coopers & Lybrand invited me to visit their offices that year. They offered me a job with the company after I graduated. This took a lot of pressure off me, but it did not stop me from making the interviewing rounds in my senior year.

I had never heard of Peat Marwick before their visit to the school, and I knew nothing about them since this was their first time coming to our campus. I was impressed with the Peat Marwick speaker, though, and the material he gave out about the firm.

In addition to Coopers & Lybrand, I decided to interview with three other firms including Peat Marwick, Price Waterhouse, and Ernst & Ernst. I was fortunate enough to be invited for office visits by all three. Each visit was an amazing experience for me. After visiting one firm, I found myself so uptight and nervous that I walked away with a major headache. At another firm, they asked me a variety of questions that made me wonder whether they were looking for a viable accounting student or a black student who would fill their quota.

For instance, I was asked if I could work in a predominately white environment. If they had reviewed my resume, they could at least have assumed that I could successfully interact with whites. I'd graduated from a predominantly white high school and served as president of the accounting society of the predominantly white university I was about to graduate from.

As it turned out, despite my concerns about the interviews, I received job offers from all three firms. I also received an updated offer from Coopers & Lybrand—giving me four offers altogether. All of this made my ultimate decision to select Peat Marwick a far more difficult one.

The Peat Marwick interview was not perfect. After lunch, job candidates would meet with the lead recruiter for the New York office and he'd give them an offer or let them know that he would be in touch in a few days, which usually meant that the job candidate would not receive an offer. However, around 2 o'clock in the afternoon, I met with the lead recruiter and was told the partner in charge of personnel for the firm wanted to meet me.

After about an hour of waiting, I was asked if I could wait about 30 more minutes since the partner was still in a meeting. Around 4 p.m., the recruiter apologized and gave me an offer. He was embarrassed and probably thought they'd blown their opportunity to recruit me. If he'd not been open with me during that two-hour waiting period and explained that the partner in charge of personnel wanted to meet me because I was black, I probably would have rejected his offer outright. But I was really impressed with what I had read about Peat Marwick; and the honesty of the recruiter helped me make up my mind to accept the offer. To this day, I have no regrets.

The salary offers I received ranged from approximately $6,500 to $7,600 annually. When I told the firm that offered me $6,500 that their offer was the lowest, they immediately matched the highest offer I had received. I saw their first offer as the true value they placed on my working for them. Their offer to me was even lower than that of a white classmate who I knew had a significantly lower grade point average than I had.

Uncle Kenneth was visiting from St. Kitts the day Peat Marwick sent me a formal letter offering me a position with the firm. I was ecstatic that I could share this good news with him, and in the back of my mind I knew he would relay it to our relatives in St. Kitts. Truthfully, I was more than a little boastful that one of the largest accounting firms in the country had courted me and made an offer so early.

I announced to everyone in the house, and anyone else within earshot, how much the company was offering me in salary. Later, after I was able to think more clearly, I regretted my behavior. There I was lording my superiority over everyone, when my aunt, who was a seamstress most of her life, and my uncle, whose life was serving as a minister, had both worked harder than I would ever work in my life and who both made a lot less money. I was ashamed of my pompous attitude and learned a hard lesson about keeping my ego in check.

When Cecelia and I visited Uncle Kenneth and his wife, Bertha, in Barbados some years later, I knew he was ill. But I had no idea just how ill. I learned shortly after arriving that he'd been diagnosed with both a heart condition and emphysema.

In time, I realized why I would always find him outside talking with Cecelia. He was actually bumming cigarettes from her, even though he knew he wasn't supposed to smoke. Aunt Bertha would fuss at him every time, but to no avail.

Toward the end of our final visit with him, he was insistent that we all sit outside. I'll never forget the beautiful view looking over the mountains and the ocean. While we all sat there appreciating the beauty of Barbados, Uncle Kenneth told me how proud he was that my brothers and I had been able to overcome so many obstacles—including the loss of our father and our mother—to achieve success. He was just as proud of his own five children. One of his sons had become a veterinarian, and the other one was a dentist. Two of his three daughters were teachers and the third became an engineer.

Uncle Kenneth's youngest daughter and my daughter, both named Michelle, were near the same age. He had advised me years ago that it was best to have children when I was young enough to enjoy them and had enough energy to keep up with them. Maybe that had something to do with my decision to get married at age 24 and have my two children by the time I was 29.

One of Uncle Kenneth's talents was painting and making plaques with inspirational quotes. During one of his trips he gave me one with the words "Never Give Up." To this day, that plaque is on my home office desk. When I'm under a lot of pressure, I often look at the plaque and somehow it helps me to deal with the problem at hand.

Uncle Kenneth knew he was dying as we sat outside that evening enjoying the scenery and talking about old times. It was the last time we would spend together. Of all the things I learned about him that evening, I was most surprised to learn that the trips we'd taken into the city all those years ago had meant as much to him as they did to me.

I began my first professional job at Peat Marwick in 1966. I was certified as a CPA from the state of New York three years later. I knew I was not among the first 100 black CPAs in the country, but I think I was perhaps among the first 125 to 150. While that was a major accomplishment for that time, it highlighted the lack of progress that blacks were making in the accounting profession.

From 1965 to 1967, most of the Big Eight accounting firms would hire one black accountant a year. No one ever told me that was the policy, but it became obvious as I met other blacks employed by these firms during this period. We also compared our offers. Once one black candidate rejected an offer, it was common practice by the firms to immediately make the offer to another black person. It was easy to confirm our suspicions by timing the rejection letters to the date the next black person was hired.

During my year as a staff accountant, I worked with great, supportive clients. Before I was assigned to an engagement, the client had to accept me. (Back in the late 1960s, I could understand this, but this practice is still used today as an excuse for not assigning blacks to certain engagements. I think that in 2006 this is ridiculous and just an excuse by the person doing the assigning.)

When I was a senior accountant, I recall one particular engagement where the client might not have known I was black. The client had just acquired a company in Norwich, Connecticut, and I was in charge of the engagement. It was a three-hour drive from New York to Norwich, which required that we stay overnight.

The president and former owner of the company was in his late 60s and had lived his entire life in this small, conservative New England town. I could tell from day one that he felt uncomfortable with me but had to accept me. He made certain that everyone cooperated with us, and the audit went very well.

At the conclusion of each audit, it was customary for the accountant to have an exit conference with the company president to discuss the results of the audit and offer recommendations. I sat down with the president to go over our findings. He showed very little interest in what I had to say. He seemed more interested in my opinions about the color he should use in painting his office.

To my surprise, once the meeting ended, he invited us to his country club for lunch. I learned later that this was his practice in previous years with white auditors. I was probably his first black guest and more than likely the first black to set foot in the country club as a guest.

The following year, I learned that when our team met with him for their audit, his first question was: "Where's that n——- that was here last year?" This is an example of the type of negative experiences minorities have had to endure and learn how to handle in order to be successful.

Over the years, I experienced many examples of what I would

describe as biases by clients trying to embarrass me in front of their board members or partners saying one thing in front of me—how good I was or how they supported my decision—then when they were among themselves, they'd say negative things about me. In some instances, those working for me as managers or staff would totally disregard my instructions.

In all of these situations I learned that I had to move above the experiences and not let them define my actions or who I was. This was the only way I knew how to succeed. An example of that happened later in my career as described by Jack Miller, a former partner at KPMG (formerly Peat Marwick):

> *"There was one incident that took place that I think paints a good picture of the kind of person Frank Ross is. A party was given in honor of Frank's predecessor as managing partner of KPMG's Washington office. This was a really big deal for Frank since it was to be the first time he would appear before the office partners as their new leader.*
>
> *"One white partner liked to take these opportunities to do a monologue—jokes where he personalized the characters. During this particular monologue, this partner joked that the firm would start serving fried chicken now that Frank had been named managing partner.*
>
> *"One of the other black partners got up and left. Other partners and their spouses were visibly upset. My understanding, however, is that Frank simply laughed and later accepted the partner's apology after so many of us told the partner his monologue had been insensitive. I can't say what Frank was really feeling or thinking, but I do know he took this opportunity of racial insensitivity—and the partner's apology—to subtlely make a statement."*

12

LAYING DOWN ROOTS IN NEW YORK

As a young married couple, Cecelia and I talked a lot about what we wanted our first home to be like. We wanted to move outside the city, so we began driving out on Saturdays, looking at houses in the suburbs. We were looking primarily in a place called Rockland County, located on the New Jersey side of the Hudson River.

If we drove too far north and saw cows, we knew we had gone too far. One Saturday we were driving around, and I saw a Peat Marwick colleague who actually worked under me. He told me he lived in the area, and we talked for a while. I remember telling him that we really liked the area and wouldn't mind living there.

Finally, after a few weeks Cecelia and I found our dream house in a subdivision that was still being built—the same subdivision that my colleague lived in. After going through the process of getting our mortgage approved, talking to the builder and choosing what we wanted in our home, the builder gave us a moving date for September. The builder had a clause in the contract that allowed him to delay the move-in date, but it prohibited us from backing out of the contract because of that delay. If we did, we would lose our down payment.

By August, we were packing up everything for the movers to take to the new house. Around that same time, we started getting phone calls from the builder asking if we would consider looking at a larger house because they were having problems finishing ours on time. We told him we were not interested, we were bent on moving into that house.

After a few more calls, we realized that there was something more to the builder's calls than just problems with the house. The next time he called, he said that because of the site our home was built on, we would likely continue to have problems with water seeping into our home, and this would cause immeasurable problems for us.

It just so happened that we had a very good lawyer who happened to be one of the first female lawyers in Yonkers. Her son was a civil engineer, and she sent him out to look at our house and check the water lines. She called us later that day and told us we had the best water flow of any of the houses in the area. After the builder realized we had a top-notch lawyer ready to take action if we needed to, he finally finished our house.

On March 15th, six months past our move-in date and the last date the builder could extend our contract, we finally moved into our home. Shortly after we moved in, we were home one day while the landscapers were finishing up the yard and the area around the house. Cecelia has always been very friendly. She started a conversation with the workers and eventually offered them a drink of Rum and Coke.

Well, as the landscapers got to know Cecelia, they became a little more talkative. Eventually, they asked Cecelia why she thought it took us so long to move into our home. Cecelia said she wasn't sure why it took so long. They told her that the builder along with the community association were working together to buy the house so we wouldn't move into their neighborhood.

These were the parents of the children who went to school and played with our children. And, more importantly, one of them was the Peat Marwick employee who worked for me. I learned that he was also one of the leaders of the association. Eventually, the employee sold his house and moved to another city farther north in Rockland County. A few years later, he also left Peat Marwick.

During the years he still lived in the neighborhood and worked with the firm, we never discussed what I went through in order to buy my home. It was the first time I really experienced housing discrimination as an adult, although I knew it existed. To actually have someone who worked for you be a part of something so blatantly racist was hard to digest.

The interesting thing about racism is that when it's brought to your attention the way it had been during our real estate experience, you begin to notice other subtle but unmistakable signs of it in your everyday life. For instance, when I took the bus from Rockland County into New York City to work, I became aware of how hesitant whites were to sit in a seat next to me. I would usually get on at the first stop and pick a window seat in either the front or middle of the bus.

By the second or third stop, almost every seat would be taken except the seat next to me. Whites would walk all the way to the rear or even stand before they would sit next to me. I always found it very amusing that these "highly educated, intelligent" business people, mostly men, would prefer to stand rather than sit next to a black person.

Sometimes I played games by making sure I was closer to the front of the bus—the second or third row—to see if the same thing would happen. When I told this to other blacks who commuted via the bus or train from Rockland or Westchester counties to New York City, they all told me they often experienced the very same thing.

After I became a partner with Peat Marwick, we ran into the same type of housing bias as before when we started looking for our second home. We would find homes we could afford in neighborhoods we wanted to move into, but the real estate people would steer us to homes we did not want, in neighborhoods we did not want to live in. We looked at beautiful homes in Long Island near where many Peat Marwick colleagues lived, but it was almost impossible to get a real estate person to show us a home there. I don't know to what extent these problems still exist, but I do know that I keep reading about the problems blacks still run into today as they try to get financing for new homes.

13

My "Star Spangled Hustle" Experience

In 1970, I was promoted to manager at Peat Marwick and two years later to senior manager. While it normally took five years to be promoted to a manager's position, I was fortunate to make manager in four years. I was one of only five others promoted with only four years experience. As I looked at the others being promoted, I realized that we all had the same kind of experience. We had all worked on major engagements and major internal projects at the firm. While some said my race was the reason my promotion came so soon in my career, I knew it was because of my performance.

In 1972, The New York Amsterdam News carried an article showing pictures of the black CPAs mainly in Eastern states. There were approximately 35 listed, and I was proud that my photo and credentials were included in that number. In many ways, that article told me that I had arrived.

During this time at Peat Marwick, I had the opportunity to manage some of the firm's largest clients, including J.C. Penney Co. I was given all the right signals that I could be a partner by 1976. Nevertheless, I left Peat Marwick to start my own firm—Ross, Stewart and Benjamin—in 1973. It was a minority CPA firm specializing in accounting and auditing of minority business enterprises; nonprofit organizations; and federal, state and local government grants. The company ultimately was made up of three principals and as many as 20 employees. We averaged $2 million to $3 million in gross annual billings during its three years in operation.

Few of my white colleagues understood why I would interrupt what looked to them like a bright future in public accounting to enter the risky landscape of business ownership. As a partner I would have had to assume a lot of responsibility that I felt I was not ready to take on. Although I had the training, I felt I did not have the real world experience others at my firm had.

In truth, there were a number of other reasons why I left Peat Marwick one year after being named a senior manager. First of all, while I knew I could become a partner, I was scared. I was 30 years old and did not have the confidence in myself that I thought was needed to be successful as a partner. Secondly, in spite of my working in a white corporate environment and having white male bosses, I never forgot my very first role model—Emsar Bradford. He was the first black CPA I had ever met, and he had a very successful practice.

As I stated earlier, Emsar Bradford made it his modus operandi to reach out to young blacks interested in the accounting field and give them encouragement every chance he got. He was, in essence, shaping future accountants. I learned a lot from him; and from that point on, I wanted to emulate him—his style, his success, his self-assurance. When I saw the car he drove, that locked the deal for me. After that, I knew that one day I would own a business and use my success to help others.

While it sounds ironic I would consider myself as both a risk taker and a very cautious person, my years in corporate America taught me that I was both and that this combination has done more to help my career than harm it.

I was at a crossroad in my career. From all appearances, I had risen to an amazing height in the white male world of public accounting. There were friends and colleagues who both admired and envied what I had achieved at that point in my career. There were mentors who had helped me get this far and couldn't imagine why I wanted to, or needed to, go someplace else. If I had been a more cautious person, rather than a risk taker, I would have thanked God and my lucky stars for my blessing and began to plan for another 20 years with Peat Marwick.

But there is another side to the Frank Ross that my friends and family know. A few people know this side—the Frank Ross who truly wants it all and is willing to work as hard as I need to to get it. That part of me was wrestling with the one who was more than grateful for what I had.

The secret that I shared with only those closest to me was that I had always wanted to own my own firm and to become as successful as Emsar Bradford appeared to be. This decision formulated shortly after I walked into Peat Marwick and learned my way around the building.

When I decided to leave Peat Marwick, I was convinced that the Nixon administration was sincere about helping blacks who were serious and committed to owning their own businesses. In my mind, it was the right time for young black executives to leave the white corporate world and try their hand at running their own businesses. The Nixon administration had even established a minority business program that would become the U.S. Small Business Administration. We were convinced that, finally, this was a vehicle to help level the economic playing field.

It was an exciting time for young women and men like me who had long been itching to own their own businesses but never felt they had the economic support necessary to take that leap. In walked the Nixon administration, promising help for those of us bold and energetic enough to put that money to good use.

It wouldn't take me long to find that there is truth to that old adage "the grass is always greener on the other side of the fence." Things out in the real world were a far cry from what I had imagined they would be. Black capitalism was, in large part, a public relations tool for then President Richard M. Nixon and his allies to win votes and make friends.

With a few exceptions, most black firms failed after a few years in operation.

Ross, Stewart and Benjamin was formed by three CPAs who met during the early years of the National Association of Black Accountants. We got along very well, and our personalities and professional skills complemented each other. Robert Stewart was a manager in the tax department of Price Waterhouse. Ronald Benjamin had left the accounting firm of Main La France to manage the internal audit department of Union Camp Inc., a Fortune 500 company in New Jersey.

As we organized ourselves, it was clear that Bob was to head our tax practice; Ron would head the audit practice and build the practice in the New Jersey area; and I would manage the practice and also perform audits. We were all going to be equally responsible for developing business.

Doug Forde, who worked for Xerox Corp. and had previously worked for Peat Marwick, also planned to join us as a partner in a year or two. He had a very extroverted personality and was to play this role when he joined us. He also had quite a few business contacts. This would have complemented my personality perfectly. However, when it was time for Doug to join us, he decided not to. This was a major blow to our long-term success.

We had secured an SBA loan immediately before my departure from Peat Marwick, but we still had to "beat the bushes" for clients. We received numerous commitment letters from firms "promising" us their business. Most times, they did not follow through. We were lucky to get a few good clients like the Jackie Robinson Foundation, headed by his widow, Rachel. She was adamant about using black firms and was a smart business woman.

We also secured the Martin Luther King Center in the Bronx, the Studio Museum of Harlem and contracts from both New York City and the state of New York. We got a few federal contracts once we got 8(a) certification from the SBA and were hired to do audits for various federal agencies. There were also a handful of minority-owned investment companies on our roster.

Still, it didn't take me long to see that the black capitalism being touted at the White House and around the country was an economic mirage. I saw firsthand how minorities were being given just enough funds to get them started, but not enough to sustain them without serious contracts from major firms. It wasn't until they went back for additional funding that these small, minority companies learned that they didn't qualify.

My partners and I cheered when we finally got through all the red tape and were certified as 8(a) small business owners—qualifying us to bid for federal government contracts. How naïve we were! There were few contracts available; and even with just a handful of black financial firms vying for the government's pot of money, it wasn't long before we learned the carrot was now even further from us—minority now included women and nonwhites of various races. Also, it was a very political process. Contracts were often given to those with the strongest political ties, which our firm did not have.

Everyone except us, it seemed, were being backed by big-moneyed husbands or partners—oftentimes large majority firms. We were at a clear disadvantage, again. Most of our clients' portfolios—all black firms— were bankrupt or on the verge of bankruptcy when they came to our firm. They simply didn't have access to the kind of capital needed to keep them afloat and viable in the competitive market.

And, truthfully, in this competitive arena there were more than a few instances of flat-out dishonest games being played with black businesses—including partners stealing from each other. One such case was a client of ours with three partners who jointly owned a very viable disco club and restaurant in a great building. They had a very successful disco clientele, although the restaurant never got up and running as they had expected. Even so, there seemed to be a discrepancy in the income they were obviously bringing in and their profit margin. We kept asking ourselves why?

Well, we finally found out. The business operated primarily on cash; and of the three principals, the two partners who had somehow not put their names on the loan were consistently at the door taking cash. The third partner, a former banker, was rarely on the club door. He was handling the business aspect of the club. The two at the door were obviously taking enough money "off the top" to leave the partnership after nine or 10 months and start their own investment banking firm on Wall Street. Sadly, those kinds of games were not unheard of in this new era of black capitalism.

On the other hand, there were many honest businesses that simply were not given the necessary funding in the first place to operate successfully. We worked with a large black-owned trucking company that was funded for long-distance hauling. It was operated by two people with extensive trucking experience, but it never got the kinds of contracts from large businesses or the federal government to sustain itself. There were just a few black businesses that survived that era—some hair care companies, *Essence* magazine, *Black Enterprise Magazine*.

As we approached many of the large black-owned businesses, it also became obvious that they were backed by white investors and politicians who wanted them to use a white CPA firm.

It was much later that I ran across Arthur I. Blaustein and Geoffrey Faux's *"The Star Spangled Hustle: The Story of a Nixon Promise."* These authors give a searing indictment of the 8(a) program and the whole black capitalism push of the 1970s. After reading their book, I felt more naïve and used than anything.

For young black entrepreneurs anxious to get in on the federal money available to small business owners, I strongly suggest they first read

Blaustein and Faux's book. The authors clearly explain how much of a game the black capitalism push really was and the relationship between white power and black capitalism. If your mind is made up about business ownership, this book won't change your mind, but it might make you cautious if you're seeking greener grass on the other side of the street.

Not only did our clients not want to always pay us for our services, but several times they also tried to have us give them certified reports without us doing the necessary work. They would come to us and tell us that in order for them to get the financing they needed to continue operations, they had to give their banker a certified audit report by the end of the week. Of course, this was not enough time for us to do the work necessary to give such an opinion. When we told them no, they would tell us that if we wanted the money owed us or wanted to continue doing their work, we would have to give them what they wanted.

During this period, I learned that there are many ways of saying no. The first is to just say no. Of course, this would mean that we would lose the client. The other was to go with the client to the banker and explain what we had to do and why it was not possible to meet the banker's demand. This was the approach we always took, and it worked in most situations. The banker would give the client a temporary advance to allow them the time that we needed to do our work.

Also, we were the last to be paid as many of our clients took us for granted. They forgot that we also had a payroll to meet. They would say to us, "You of all people know my cash position."

I learned a lot through this experience about small business ownership, about U.S. capitalism and about myself. I realized after a time that there was no large pool of "minority business" out there. I also learned that my personality was not suited for business development. I am not a person who can walk into a room of potential businesses and make it happen. I couldn't make that initial contact. None of us at the firm had that skill. I was the person to come in after the initial contact had been made. Then, I could almost guarantee a contract.

After these experiences, and the introspection, I began to ask myself serious questions about remaining with our firm. My first effort was to bring in someone else who I knew would be good for our operation.

Bert Mitchell, a partner with Lucas Tucker—the largest black-owned CPA firm in the New York area—had just left the company and opened his own firm. Bert was the 100th CPA in the country, becoming certified by the state of New York in 1965. Bert also had a very extroverted personality. He was a few years older and had many of the political connections I thought were necessary for the success of any black-owned firm. In short, he had many of the skills I lacked.

While I was pretty sure Bert and I would consummate a deal and together build a successful firm, little did I know that there was another firm courting him at the same time. He ended up bringing in the partner from this other firm to form Mitchell Titus, which today is recognized as one of the largest black-owned CPA firms in the United States.

Several years later, my former firm—Ross, Stewart and Benjamin—merged with Mitchell Titus, and one of my former partners is still a partner in Mitchell Titus. If Bert and I had been successful in joining forces at the time, I probably would never have returned to Peat Marwick.

I found that while my weakness was making the initial contact, one of my strengths became very clear—my ability to close deals. I was able to do this because of my listening skills—that is, listening to what people wanted and then tailoring my services in a way that would help them achieve their goals. Also, I realized that people trusted me.

While I was at Peat Marwick, I never really had to develop business. The potential client either came to us because of the name Peat Marwick or because of a relationship they had with a partner. Of course, this was not the case with Ross, Stewart and Benjamin. Also, since I gave the appearance of being a quiet person, many people interpreted that as a sign of weakness and tried to take advantage of me.

I'm a strong believer in sticking to my commitments, but I also believe in reading the handwriting on the wall. Even when I was three years into the business and quickly becoming disillusioned, I was torn by my innate need to succeed and to stick to this commitment I had made to myself and my partners. I began thinking strategically about how to move the business forward. I realized that the only way was to utilize our 8(a) certification. I was completely turned off by the thought of getting deeply involved in federal government red tape. My experience was that the people working in government were forever seeking to "teach me" things I already knew about my field of work.

In the midst of this mental and emotional turmoil, I received a call from a Peat Marwick partner who said he had heard I was looking to leave my practice. I told him that was not in my plans. The wheels of my return to Peat Marwick had all started when Richard Clarke, a well-known black New York headhunter I had known over the years, sent an old resume to Equitable Life—a major insurance company.

Richard had gotten hold of one of my old resumes but called me to ask for an updated version to send to Equitable, which was searching for the number two person in internal auditing who would head internal audit within a year or two. I started to tell him I wasn't interested but then decided it wouldn't hurt. It was fairly common practice in the public accounting field to float resumes around, even if you have no intention of leaving your current position.

I figured I probably wouldn't hear back from them anyway. I was wrong. It turned out that Equitable Life called my old bosses at Peat Marwick for a reference. A few days later, I received a call from Peat Marwick's partner in charge of the New York office's personnel department. My friends and I still joke that I might have ended up with

Equitable Life if they hadn't seen the need to check up on me by calling Peat Marwick that early in the process.

I finally decided to return to Peat Marwick and settled inside myself that I had not failed but had taken the best option available at the time. I conceded that I had made two of the most significant decisions of my life within those three years. The first good decision was to leave Peat Marwick and strike out on my own. The second was my decision to return to Peat Marwick.

I learned a lot more about myself and about running a business in that environment than I ever would have learned as a manager at Peat Marwick. I discovered that I was better suited for the big firm's environment and that government auditing was not for me. If I had not left Peat Marwick when I did, though, I would always ask myself "what if?"

In truth, the experience made me a lot more confident, which I felt would result in a much more successful manager and partner for Peat Marwick. I was able to return to Peat Marwick with full knowledge of my strengths and weaknesses. I had done all I could to make a success of the business, and I simply didn't have all the answers. I came back stronger, with a broader knowledge of business in general and of the accounting field—and with a more realistic sense of my abilities. I was proud of myself for taking the chance, and I learned a great deal from the experience. I could say, for certain, that I had gotten the desire to run my own firm out of my system.

14

MAKING PARTNER—BAPTISM BY FIRE

In 1977, 10 years after I went to work at Peat Marwick, I became the first and only black partner at the firm. It was during a time when government and private firms were trying to do the "right" thing when it came to race. The national office in New York made a point of releasing photos of their new black partner to the local and national media outlets. I was the first African-American partner in the firm out of approximately 1,000 partners throughout the country.

That same year, I was invited to my very first partners' meeting, and I learned firsthand just how true that old saying, "It's lonely at the top," really was. The 1977 partners' meeting was held at the Boca Raton Hotel and Golf Club in beautiful Boca Raton, Florida. While I had always heard about these meetings, I was excited about learning whether they were everything people had said they were. I found out very early on that they were all that and more.

Partners would fly into Miami, Fort Lauderdale or West Palm Beach from different parts of the country. We had offices in each of these cities, and the staff would meet us at the airport and show us to our waiting limousines. In later years, when the number of partners significantly increased, some of them would gripe about not being met by limousines or having to travel by air-conditioned bus.

The meetings always lasted four days, beginning on a Tuesday or what we called our "travel day." The hospitality suite was open and at full throttle as soon as we arrived. There was a full menu at mealtimes, including an extensive wine list. Over the years, this was sometimes abused. Eventually the list of entrees decreased, and wine was placed on tables beforehand.

There was a lodging hierarchy. If you found yourself housed in the Towers, you knew you had "arrived" since these were reserved for the heavy hitters. The main building had deep oriental rugs and an ocean view. The rooms in the main hotel, except some rooms on the ground floor which originally were designed as servants' quarters, were spacious and elegantly decorated. Since I was new, I was assigned to the ground floor of the main building. Some partners were housed in villas which required ground transportation to get to the main building.

Any resident of the resort was treated royally. But the partners were treated best, by far. We filled the entire resort, and the firm paid for everything—lodging, meals, drinks, golf, tennis, deep-sea fishing and tips. While most of the partners golfed or played tennis, I went fishing. I found it extremely relaxing, and it got me away from the "mad house."

Boca had something for everyone—a golf course on the premises and two other championship golf courses at Boca West which had its own opulent dining room. There were tennis courts, the beach, 40-foot-plus sport fishermen cruisers for deep-sea fishing and three bars. One bar, overlooking the ocean, had entertainment nightly.

The closing night of the meeting was always a black-tie dinner where retiring partners were honored along with the winners of the golf, tennis and bridge tournaments.

I came to the partners meeting with a major handicap—I did not play poker, and poker was a critical part of the four days we spent in Boca Raton. Imagine, more than a thousand partners in and out of what we called "the game room" all night. There was a variety of levels of tables— from just a few dollars to thousands of dollars. There was one table that was considered the "regulars." I have never been a gambler, and I couldn't imagine a person sitting down at a game and losing hundreds, sometimes thousands of dollars in one sitting!

For all those years as a partner, I missed out on what most people considered the most exciting part of the meeting. The poker games were full service with waiters, a bar—and maybe most importantly, there was the opportunity to rub shoulders and network with the head honchos at the firm. Poker games lasted every night of the four-day meeting from 8 or 9 o'clock in the evening to 4 or 5 o'clock in the morning . . . and on the last night of the meeting, sometimes they lasted until noon the next day.

Whatever arrogance, pride and elation I had over my new-found opportunity to rub elbows with the upper crust of Peat Marwick was dashed during my first partners' meeting. If I had ever thought for a moment that I was special because I was the first or only black to infiltrate this close-knit, predominantly white fraternity, I would think again after that week. You had to have been there to understand. Several white colleagues—fellow partners from all over the country—made it unapologetically clear to me that week in beautiful Boca Raton that I was not wanted in their fraternity. Several partners had already, in fact, gone on record saying they would never have a black partner in their firm. You can imagine their surprise when they saw me at the meeting.

It was certainly one of the lowest moments of my career at Peat Marwick—the first time I'd actually felt unwelcome by my colleagues... as if I didn't belong. I was called racist names to my face—some I had heard and several I had never heard even on the schoolyards of Yonkers. One partner would start the taunting, and others would jump in. They felt absolutely comfortable treating a fellow partner like an intruder who had no reason to be there.

Some partners watched and listened to this totally unnecessary abuse, then walked away, not saying a word in my defense and averting their eyes from me. I ignored it all to the extent that I could and forced myself not to respond to even the worst taunting. The hatred and prejudice were palpable; but somewhere deep inside I also knew it was fear and a feeling of losing control on their part. I remember thinking, "If this is what it takes for you to live with me . . . ." I forced myself to hear it and not hear it, but above all not to let my temper turn their hate into my undoing.

Certain partners would always find something stereotypical to say to depersonalize me. Many people said I looked a lot like Reggie Jackson, the baseball player. The partners would make insulting remarks about that, about his baseball record—anything to make me feel less than them.

Back at the firm, I threw myself into my work trying to forget what happened. None of my colleagues ever brought up the incident. I guess I was naïve, expecting fellow partners who I had considered friends or mentors to approach me and apologize for what happened. Eventually, I was able to put it in the "past" file, viewing it as simply one of the not-so-pretty snapshots of the path up the corporate ladder.

I was approached by a young black manager who was excited to hear all about the partners' meeting. After a brief discussion, he quickly sensed my disappointment. When I told him what had happened, he reassured me that I could not give in to this type of treatment; that I had to rise above it.

Sometimes I still try to dissect it, justify it—understand how "good" people lose what redeeming qualities they have in the midst of a group like that. While there were no New York partners at the event, several members of the firm's leadership were there and the fact that they did not set the standard of acceptance told me something that I did not like to think much about.

The next year I attended the partners meeting there were some taunting, abuse, but not as much. Within a few years, it stopped altogether. My colleagues, some new and some who had been there from the beginning, acted as if it had never happened. By the early 1980s, there were several black partners, and no one would have dared be as open with their prejudice or racism when there were more than one.

Even after that rough spot had blown over, I would continue to run into signs that some white partners did not believe I belonged, did not think I had paid my dues to be a part of their fraternity. With age and more confidence in myself, I began to attach those kinds of feelings to the person who carried them, not to me. I saved myself a lot of stress that way.

In the later years, I slowly began to assimilate into the partner's mode during these annual events. While I was not a heavy drinker or party person, I ended up doing more than my share of both. It was only with a concerted effort that I was able to hold onto who I was and not be seduced by the camaraderie that comes with being a part of such an august fraternity.

One year, I invited Cecelia to meet me in Miami after the annual meeting. She came down on a Friday to spend the weekend. To surprise me, she reserved a beautiful suite—seeing it as an opportunity for us to get away from the kids and home life and enjoy a romantic weekend with just the two of us. But by the time I finally got to the hotel mid-Saturday morning, all I could do that day and the next day was "recover" from my night with the partners. Cecelia was livid! That was the last time we tried hitching a romantic weekend on the same ticket as the partners' meeting.

In 1981, Sheila Clark became the second partner of color and the first black woman partner. When Sheila attended her first partners' meeting, I remember hearing about this young female partner from the Houston office who won most of the money at the Tuesday night high-stakes poker games. I knew that Sheila had "arrived" and was putting her stamp on the partners' meeting.

During the early 1980s, more blacks were starting to be admitted into the partnership at the firm. There was a small group of us who became very close. The story that seems to never die is about how we had long awaited enough members to start our own Bid Whist game. The card room was "by invitation only," and to get in you either had to be invited by longtime game members or have enough in your group to play a game.

By 1984, we finally had a fourth partner for the card game. We were all ecstatic! There were Sheila Clark, Larry Bailey, Eddie Munson and me. In all of our excitement, however, we overlooked one important fact—we had four players, but only three could play Bid Whist. For some unknown reason, I had never shared with the group that I never learned to play Bid Whist. Needless to say, it was another few years of waiting before the fifth black partner, LaMar Swinney, came along. Thank goodness he was a great Bid Whist player!

"Most people seek mentors at a very senior level . . . . The best mentors are not always high up. One of the things I have been able to do is form some mentor relationship with people who were relatively low in the company structure but whom I admired for how they operated and what they stood for. They gave me incredible advice and said to me . . . 'The issue is not forming a strong personal relationship. That's fine if it comes, but the way to form a mentor relationship is to network off your performance . . . . Choose mentors you admire and want to emulate.' "

—Ken Chenault
President and CEO
American Express
(Excerpt from Knowledge@Wharton Journal)

The road leading
to Monkey Hill in
St. Kitts

The Ross family's home
on Market Street circa 1940s

Monkey Hill in St. Kitts

St. Georges Anglican Church
where Frank was christened
in St. Kitts

Reginald Ross, Frank's father

The Ross boys in
St. Kitts, before
moving to the
United States:
(l to r) Winston, Willie,
Frank and Clarence

The Ross boys with Aunt
Florence shortly after
arriving in New York:
(l to r) Clarence, Winston,
Frank and Willie

SCHOOL No. 5
DEC. 6, 1955   CLASS 6S

Frank (seated far left on third row)
at School No. 5 in Yonkers, N.Y.

Frank's mother Ruby (far right) along with (l to r) Eulie,
Eulie's mother Etta and Eulie's sister Rhoda. (One of the
few pictures of Frank's mother later in life.)

Frank with Auntie
in 1963 before
she became ill

A young Auntie during her
early years in New York

Frank and Cousin
Eulie

Cecelia at age 19
when she and Frank first met

The Ross brothers' last photo before Clarence's death:
(l to r) Winston, Frank, Willie and Clarence

Auntie (center) at
Cecelia's college
graduation with (l to r)
Cecelia's father,
Cecelia, Cecelia's mother and
grandmother

Cecelia's high
school graduation
picture

Frank and his family (l to r):
Michael, Frank, Cecelia and Michelle

Frank volunteering
at a soup kitchen
in Washington

(Above) Frank
presenting
an award
on behalf of
Iona Senior
Services to
D.C. Mayor
Sharon Pratt
Kelley

(Right) Frank
makes a
presentation
to D.C. students
at a Hoop Dreams
reception. Hoop
Dreams Director
Susie Kay is
standing nearby
(far left).

Frank with five of the nine NABA founders:
(seated l to r) Donald Bristow, Daniel Moore
(the current president) and Ronald Benjamin;
(standing l to r) frank Ross, Bert Gibson,
Earl Biggett and Michael Winston

Frank with former KPMG Washington office
managing partners (from left) Tony Natelli,
Dave Fowler, Frank and James T. Boyle

15

MENTORING: THE CRITICAL MISSING PIECE

Any successful man or woman who tells you they have made it on their own either has a faulty memory or a jaundiced view of life . . . or maybe they have a very narrow view of who and what a mentor really is. What I know and what I tell young people seeking advice about their careers is that choosing the right mentor, nurturing that relationship and treating that relationship with honesty and integrity is as important to a successful journey as choosing the right company or department within a company.

Without question, mentoring is critical to a successful career. It was very critical to my own success at several stages in my career. It is something, however, that you cannot force. It has to happen naturally. I have seen, far too often, corporate leaders with good intentions "assign" mentors to new employees as if the assignment dictates a true bonding experience. What I have found over and over is that this forced mentoring is rarely effective or long lasting. I agree that it serves a purpose, but it should not be mistaken as a true mentoring relationship. It is more a counseling-type relationship.

Mentoring comes from a sincere desire to help guide another's journey through sharing one's own experiences, knowledge and life lessons. The hope is that through sharing, the "mentee" will avoid some of the errors or pitfalls experienced by the mentor. When the mentoring relationship comes out of that sincerity and when the recipient is open and honest, there will always be some modicum of success.

I am especially proud of the Howard University Center for Accounting Education's Leadership Development Program. This mentoring project grew out of a commitment by several accounting firms, both large and small, to contribute to developing young accounting professionals of color and from my own desire to give back and to share my experiences with youth interested in going into the accounting field.

While it was not an overnight success, it was a sincere commitment; and without that sincere commitment a mentorship program won't be effective. My commitment was a desire to steer young accounting professionals into healthy networking situations so they would not experience the loneliness and isolation that many corporate accountants of color experienced during the last three decades when we sat alone on our floors, in the boardrooms, in the pristine corporate buildings.

In truth, there is a little bit of selfishness in mentoring to the extent that the mentor is helping people achieve success, and the hope is that they will pass that on to someone else. Our legacies are built on people we touch in our lives, and great legacies are built on the great people we helped along the way.

The mentee also has a responsibility, which can be summed up in one word—deliver. The mentee must do his or her best to perform at an outstanding level.

Ironically, most of my early mentors were African Americans, while my professional and career mentors have practically all been white men. That's not to overlook the whites who helped me in my early life or the blacks who made a significant difference in my journey during my career. What is true, though, is that I grew up in a mostly black world until my teen and college years; then I moved into a mostly white world—at least during my prescribed eight-plus hours at the office.

It should not be difficult to understand, either, that those in positions to mentor young accountants were the white men who held positions of power in my and so many other accounting firms. The other side of that truth is that even in 1966, I was the second black professional to join Peat Marwick in its almost 80-year history. For many years I was the highest-ranking black in any of the other major accounting firms worldwide.

I say this not to toot my own horn, but to make two points: 1) My mentorships, if there were to be any, were dependent on the goodness of powerful white men already there; and 2) Today's young professionals should keep in the utmost of their minds as they move up the career ladder that being the "first" is good and fine, but continuously being the "only" is nothing the accounting community or we should still be proud of.

Blacks who are achieving success should reach back and help younger blacks in the profession just as those powerful white men did with me as I was advancing upward in the accounting profession. As we succeed, we have to mentor others as well.

Many young blacks who I mentored during my career have used this to become successful—many of them more successful than I became. But I also cannot forget those who looked at my helping them as a way to take advantage of our relationship and not perform.

Elaine Hart, my former administrative assistant, recalled one such incident in particular:

> "There was one group of new hires that came in, including quite a few African Americans, one year. And I don't know what it was about this group, but whenever things didn't go their way, they would use the race card. They expected that because Frank Ross was black, he would support them, but he wouldn't. At first, I wondered why Frank didn't step up for them, too.
>
> "After we talked, I fully understood his rationale. He told me they were not holding up their end of the bargain. He had had meetings with them, and their work was substandard.

"One young man came in and talked with him. Frank told him that he couldn't use the race card every time things don't go the way he wants. Before pulling the race card, he said, make sure it's a race issue. In this case, the youngster simply wasn't performing up to the firm's expectations and then questioned why he wasn't getting the good clients. But when he was given the good clients, he wasn't performing.

"The advice Frank gave him was: 'You will always be under the microscope in corporate America. The only way you'll make it in this environment is to consistently cross every T and dot every I, in spite of what everyone else does or gets away with not doing.' He told him that he had been given an opportunity that few people got and that if he blew it, it would follow him.

"It is very impressive to say you work at KPMG. It is so important coming into a place like this to have a mentor, and Frank served as a mentor for blacks and whites. He tried to work with that group of young people and impress upon them that theirs wouldn't be an easy job but that once they proved themselves it gets a lot easier. Even now, Frank serves as a mentor to a lot of people in this field, and he has helped a lot of people's careers."

When I first arrived at Peat Marwick, I was filled with awe, pride and a whole lot of fear. Would I measure up? Would my colleagues view me as simply a colleague and judge my work, not my race? Would I be able to move up in the firm? That was something I wanted from the beginning.

Luckily, I met someone early on at the firm who I would later refer to as my earliest mentor. Here I was, fresh in this big company and I already had someone looking out for me, offering me an opportunity. That person was Sy Bohrer, the first Jewish partner at Peat Marwick.

When I joined the firm in 1966, Sy Bohrer was already one of the most successful New York office partners. He had built a very successful practice around the New York-based entertainment, advertising and publishing industries.

Sy was one of those people who helped my career without my knowing that he was helping. As I look back on my first four years on the staff, I worked mostly on engagement in Sy's group. When I wasn't working on his engagement, I worked on audits of stockbrokerage companies.

On Sy's engagement, I was always assigned to challenging roles and was constantly having to prove how good I was. For that matter, I was put in charge of my first audit by the end of my first year. This was very rarely done back in those days. This helped me work harder and allowed me to constantly learn new things. The people working on these engagements were tough, but they were the best. Had it not been for this experience during my early years, I doubt if I would have been as successful.

I will never forget Sy telling me: "Frank, you can't ever be afraid to make a decision . . . just know that you'll be right 90 percent of the time; and when the person making the final decision disagrees with you, it's not always because you're wrong. But the reason they disagree might just be that they want to choose another option." I give Sy a lot of credit for being what I would call a "silent mentor."

I ended up working on many of Sy's major engagements—United Artists, Revlon, several publishing companies including Westchester Rockland Newspapers (now Gannett) and a few Madison Avenue advertising companies. The interesting thing was that these accounts were all part of his practice. He did not have to assign me to these accounts. What that told me was that Sy had decided he would bring me under his wing and give me a chance to prove myself. I was new to the firm, and that was a big risk he took.

When I advanced to the management group, I met James (Jim) T. Powers who became a very important mentor. Jim was a red-haired

Southerner from Atlanta. The name "redneck" would have fit Jim perfectly, not just because he was a Southerner with red hair, but because he also played high stakes cards, smoked cigars and enjoyed a good drink. Jim's strength was his people skills, and it was through him that I learned how to appreciate client service and how to cultivate good relationships with people working with me.

When I first met Jim, he was the partner in charge of the firm's merchandising practice. He was a recognized leader in the accounting industry. When I was promoted to manager, I was assigned to his group. From day one, I was given challenging assignments and the opportunity to gain confidence by developing merchandising training programs and assisting Jim in writing books on the retail inventory method.

It seemed from the beginning that Jim was grooming me to move up in the firm. In addition to developing the retail training program for the firm, I was also given instructing responsibilities at several of the firm's accounting training programs, which gave me lots of exposure and helped build my self-confidence.

Jim also allowed me to become the engagement manager on the J.C. Penney account, one of the firm's largest accounts at the time. That showed me that he thought I knew what I was doing and that he was confident that I wouldn't let him down.

Jim taught without lecturing or preaching. He taught me by example how to delegate responsibility, while maintaining overall responsibility of one's team decision. Following his example, I gained the confidence I needed to make decisions and to stick by them.

While Jim, on the surface, fit the stereotypes of the white southern male, below the surface there was nothing further from that stereotype. The most lasting lesson I learned from him was not to judge the book by the cover.

When I left Peat Marwick, Jim was one of the people who thought I was making a mistake, but he also told me to call him if I ever decided to come back. During the time I was trying to decide whether to return to Peat Marwick, he and I met for dinner several times and discussed the pros and cons of my decision. When I finally decided that returning to the firm was the best thing for my family, Jim was the first one to encourage me to do so. He told me I should plan to come back right away, rather than wait until later.

"You should make the move now, rather than later," he said. "The people there already know you and your work. They can support your coming back because of their firsthand knowledge. If you wait, the people making that decision might not be the same."

There were a lot of subtle lessons Jim taught me. There was one particular incident at a party where, like most times, I was the only black person present. A white temporary secretary had been invited. She was a very attractive young woman, and she spent most of that evening blatantly flirting with me—not in a subtle way at all. When I look back, I realize that it must have been obvious to just about anyone there what was going on. But for my part, I didn't reciprocate. I simply kept talking as if I didn't notice what she was doing.

The next day, Jim stopped me at the elevator and told me it was very obvious what was happening at the party the night before. He said I had handled the situation the right way. Without saying a lot more, he told me that no matter where you are, you have to always be mindful that there will be someone watching how you handle yourself. I never forgot that, and I am sure his advice has saved me from encountering many problems in my career.

I had worked extensively for Jim before leaving the firm, and when I returned I worked with him again, but in a different position. This time, we worked together as colleagues.

Dan Robinson was another mentor who played an important role in my career. Dan was responsible for the higher education and nonprofit audit department. We became very good friends, and I learned a great deal from him about client relationships. He was great with clients, and for this field that is probably the most important part of one's job.

Most likely, none of these men ever realized how much they helped my career, but in their own unique ways they did a great deal to make my path up the corporate ladder less rocky. I would even guess that one or two of them might have believed that I would have made it with or without their help. Thank goodness, I didn't have to find out if that was true or not.

The fact is, none of these people was asked to mentor me to the extent that they did. And what I learned from those relationships was that I had a responsibility, too. Just as the mentors reached out—sometimes taking a risk by giving me a chance—I had a responsibility not to bungle that opportunity or take advantage of their kindness.

This is even more important for young African Americans who come into a firm under the mentorship of a black manager or executive. It is so important that "mentees" handle that relationship with respect and integrity—by keeping their ends of the bargain; by honoring their commitments; and by all means, not causing their mentors to risk their own job stability.

Sadly, I have personal experiences of young professionals who waste bright futures and invaluable opportunities by devaluing their mentor relationships. I cannot count on two hands the number of youth I have had to remind that the race card will only get you so far in corporate America. In the end, the ability to do your job is what counts. There's no question that a strong mentoring relationship helps.

16

FROM THE BIG APPLE TO CHOCOLATE CITY

I had been a partner in the New York office for two years, working in not-for-profit, healthcare and retailing/merchandising departments of the audit practice when I was asked to transfer to Peat Marwick's Washington office. It was 1979, and I was comfortable in my role as a young partner with a great future ahead of me. Cecelia and I were also talking seriously about buying our second home. This one, she said, would be her dream home.

We were both settling into our lives. Our son Michael was now in nursery school. And after 13 years of putting her career on hold, Cecelia was able to focus on her own career again. She was scheduled to graduate from Dominican College with her bachelor's degree in social work and had been accepted to Hunter College's master's program for social work. In addition, she had landed a job that she was very excited about.

Little did I know that the D.C. office was already talking to the New York office about the possible transfer of a partner with public service experience. Of course, my name was one being actively discussed. Cecelia and I had both agreed that the last place either of us expected to, or wanted to, move to was Washington, D.C. or any other city below the Mason-Dixon Line.

As it turned out, the day after I mentioned to the partner in charge of the nonprofit practice that Cecelia and I were about to consummate the contract for our new home, I was called into the managing partner's office and offered the opportunity to transfer to Washington. My understanding from that conversation was that the D.C. office had lost a major nonprofit client and was having trouble completing an audit of Howard University. This was creating havoc for the D.C. office's critical relationship with the university.

The D.C. office also had a new managing partner, Steve Harlan, who was responsible for my pivotal move from New York to Washington. Steve had decided that the public sector, especially the nonprofit community, represented a great opportunity for growth. I had all the qualities one could ask for in a partner to work in the D.C. office— African American with extensive experience working in the entire public sector arena. Steve told me I did not have to give him an answer that day.

It was during this time that I had doubts as to whether the CEO of J.C. Penney would accept me as his peer. I knew he would accept me as a solid accountant, a Peat Marwick partner . . . but that would be it. The heads of the public sector clients, I was convinced, would more readily accept me as their peer. I felt this was important if I was going to be successful in the long run.

I discussed this with Jim Powers, the partner in charge of the merchandising practice and someone I considered a mentor. Jim disagreed with me. He was certain that as I grew older and gained experience, the CEOs of major corporations such as J.C. Penney would accept me and seek me out to discuss their problems like any other senior partner. He assured me I did not have to accept the offer to move to D.C., and he discussed future opportunities available to me in New York. He even outlined a possible scenario of how it could all happen. I could achieve my goal—becoming more than just a line partner—if I stayed in New York. This made my choice even more difficult.

But I chose to accept the move to Washington, even though the reputation of D.C. placed it on the bottom of my list of cities where I wanted to work. This was one of those cases when you don't have to always follow the advice of your mentor. In the end, you have to make the decisions that are best for you. This was one of them.

I practiced all the way home how I would tell Cecelia. The way I presented the news to her, however, was as a question: Which city was it that we both agreed we did not want to move to? She immediately knew the answer. Cecelia and I had both known that I might eventually have to move to advance in my career. We had ranked the cities we thought African-American partners would most likely be asked to move to . . . and D.C. almost always was the last on our list.

Cecelia was angrier and unhappier about this than I had expected her to be. This was probably the closest thing to serious marital strife she and I would ever have. I understood Cecelia's dismay. She was just beginning to get her life back, where she wasn't just Mrs. Frank Ross. Our daughter, Michelle, was just going into the sixth grade and loved her school and her friends. Michael wasn't as much of a problem, since he was not yet in grade school. Besides, my son made friends faster than anyone I had ever met, and I knew it wouldn't be hard for him to adapt to any new community.

Neither Cecelia, nor I relished leaving the proximity of our families. New York was all Cecelia had ever known, and truthfully it encompassed most of my memories as well. I know Cecelia would never admit it, but I'm convinced that the one thing that finally pushed her to close her eyes and pack her bags was her girlfriends telling her that the female/male ratio was 10-to-1 in the so-called "Chocolate City" and that the women were very pretty and very aggressive. It was not long after that conversation that she finally acquiesced to leaving her exciting New York and moving to D.C., which she was convinced was the same as moving "down South."

I wasn't eager to move, either. However, after putting the pluses and minuses on paper, I decided that this would be a great opportunity since

I wanted to eventually get into the management aspect of the firm. I could not see that happening in the New York office. I always thought that to be a successful partner you needed to be accepted by the CEOs of your major clients as their equal—on equal footing.

In the end, I decided to accept the transfer. By July 1979, we had moved. I would not admit it to Cecelia, but there was more than a smattering of excitement about the possible challenges that lay ahead. There were more personal pluses, too. Even Cecelia had to agree I could never arrive home for a 6 o'clock dinner in New York—unless I left my office at 3 p.m. or 4 p.m.!

We bought our home during a weekend visit. The community we settled on—Potomac, Maryland, just outside the D.C. city limits—was a beautiful, residential community. And our home cost a lot less than that same home would have cost in a comparative area in New York.

There were three other partners moving from the New York office to Washington during the same time as we were. One partner had moved six months earlier, and we used his real estate agent. We were very happy with her. Once we gave her our criteria—telling her she need not show us any homes in Virginia—she showed us exactly what we asked for. We chose the Potomac area both because of the community and the schools. We were amazed and relieved at the contrast between New York's real estate experience and our experience in D.C.

It was our second Potomac home—just blocks from the first one—that would become Cecelia's dream home. It was, indeed, a magnificent home built by noted D.C. architect Roy Mason. Cecelia turned over the interior design to Barbara Campbell of Persimmon Tree Designs. Cecelia swears the home exemplifies my complex personality—unassuming from the outside, yet a completely different story from the inside.

Almanac columnist Robert Reed, who wrote a series called "By Design," came out shortly after we had moved in and did an exclusive interview on us and our home. He called our new abode "self-contradictory." And like most people who walk into the front door of our home, he was not prepared for the contrast of the outside and inside. He was especially mesmerized by our growing collections of art and music.

Steve Harlan had understood our reticence about relocating to D.C. and spent a lot of time and effort trying to make sure Cecelia and I felt welcome once we had made the move.

Steve was not a micromanager. Instead, he gave me the freedom I needed to be successful in achieving my goal of building a public sector practice. Maybe his most valuable contribution to my growth was in helping me understand the importance of getting to know the clients, developing relationships and building those relationships into successful business opportunities.

Whenever I encountered client problems early on, I could always count on Steve to support me. He demanded a lot from me and the rest of his staff, but he never left me to handle a problem by myself.

Joe Boyle, partner at the D.C. office, also helped make our move less traumatic. Joe, along with Steve, had been anxiously awaiting my arrival. Both went out of their way to make me feel welcome in the new office. Cecelia and I got to know their wives and went to dinner with them a few times. To be truthful, after a few weeks of learning my way around the new workplace, I accepted my fate, fell into my job and allowed it to pretty much become my second life.

It took me a while to settle into my new role and my new environment. While the opportunity to lead the public sector division was a great one, I had never partnered a black-owned-or-operated client in the New York office. Now, I was partner on the Howard University account—one of the D.C. office's major clients. Howard University and another community-based organization were significant to the office's success. However, they had not received the service they deserved from our office.

My move brought with it a number of rumors and office politics. One rumor was that I was moved to D.C. because I "couldn't cut the mustard." Another was that I would soon be leaving the firm. I became incensed by the joke going around the office that Peat Marwick had traded a senior manager from the D.C. office for my transfer to D.C.

In the New York office, I had never had to deal with being considered for black clients simply because I was black. I had handled diverse clients, not just blacks. But I soon found that in D.C. this was pretty much a given. It was common to be asked to service a client because they happen to be black.

Even today, tokenism is accepted in D.C. and likely the reason the real power is not in the black communities, in spite of the fact the city has a predominantly black population. I also never heard it "articulated" in New York that a client would not accept blacks on their accounts. In D.C., it was openly discussed.

I had to come to grips with the fact that it had nothing to do with me, but the environment I was now working in. In those situations, I would always make certain I played a meaningful role and was involved in a meaningful way. If it turned out that I would not be significantly involved, I would not work with the client.

As I was learning my new environment, I realized the move was traumatic for Cecelia. I was grateful for the few partners' wives who took Cecelia under their wings, helping in her introduction to the area.

One of those women was Ann Kilcullen, whose husband, Tim, also transferred from New York. Tim had worked in the D.C. office as a consulting partner for quite a while. The other woman was Susan Brita, who was married to an audit partner, Ernie, who also transferred from the New York office a year earlier to handle financial service clients. Ann and Susan would regularly invite Cecelia out to lunch or dinner, and eventually Cecelia was able to build up her own network of friends.

Denise Johnson was another person who helped make Cecelia's transition from New York much smoother. She was the wife of a black manager who transferred to the New York office. Without the support of these partners and managers' wives, I wonder if Cecelia would have moved back to New York. Oftentimes, as professionals move from one location to another, we forget how important it is to make sure spouses are not forgotten.

One of the black managers who was also very instrumental in helping us adjust to life in the D.C. area was Larry Bailey. Larry was a young manager in the tax department at the time of my transfer. He was well-connected in the D.C. business community, having grown up in the area. He, and later his new wife, Loleta, became part of our social group and our family. Larry and Cecelia always teased Loleta and me about our seriousness. Even our children became an active part of the foursome. Larry also introduced me into the right business circles which was very helpful in my new role. He ultimately became the third black partner in Peat Marwick.

My son Michael had no problem adjusting to his new home, but my daughter Michelle had a tougher time adjusting. She was older and more vested in her friends and school in New York. It took five years for D.C. to grow on Cecelia. Family members all joked that she was the epitome of a New York socialite, and she swore I had kidnapped her and brought her to the brink of hell. D.C. was definitely not New York, but I told her it wasn't quite that bad. In fact, after getting use to the slower pace and the bureaucratic gridlock that's still so much a part of the fabric of the U.S. capital, the move proved to be an exciting new phase of my corporate career.

My faith has always been an enormously important part of my life and my journey since I moved to the States. It has given me a certain amount of comfort and peace and quiet I've always needed to ground myself and do the work I have to do. No matter what's happening around me, what the obstacles are, my faith has always gotten me through it.

What I never discussed with many people is how my move to D.C. paralleled with a troubling lapse in my faith. In retrospect, this was likely also influenced by my concern to fit into my new environment. While I had joined a small neighborhood church much like the one I'd been accustomed to attending in New York, I later began visiting larger churches in downtown D.C.

After a time, I gradually stopped attending church altogether. During this phase in my life, I began to notice something different about my persona. I was becoming a much more negative person. I'd been able to ignore so much going on around me through the years while still realizing that the negative existed. But I was always able to move forward without dwelling on it. Suddenly, I was being stagnated by my focus on the negative.

It was a year or two later that I realized how, in leaving behind my faith, I was leaving behind the part of me that had been critical in my successes and achievements. I realized that I had somehow gotten off track and that this new person I thought might fit better in my new environment wouldn't at all work for me. It wasn't who I was.

A friend counseled me, saying he believed my lapse in faith was affecting me in a much more profound way than I imagined; that my faith had over the years grounded me. I was also told of a small A.M.E. Zion church in Rockville, Maryland, which I began attending.

I have long had a deep interest in religion and how people's faith manifests itself in their everyday lives. While I'm now grounded in my faith, I'm also conscious of people's conservative views of their religion being the one and only. I encounter many people of faith who hold such strict interpretations of the Bible. Though I grew up under my uncle's near-fanatical religious restrictions, as I grew older I was able to put religion into perspective. I don't use it as a crutch or an excuse to duck out on life.

The D.C. office was significantly smaller, with unique problems of its own. It wasn't long before I realized that this was an opportunity for me to prove my worth and to reach success. The marketplace also offered a great opportunity for me to build a successful practice.

Steve Harlan was making critical changes and bringing in partners to handle each of those changes. I was the not-for-profit quarterback who would successfully re-establish credibility within the community and recruit several new major not-for-profit clients. These wins had nothing to do with race.

The Public Broadcasting Service was probably the largest of these early wins. What made this win interesting was our proposal. The PBS proposal was my first opportunity to work on a major pitch to a major new client. Considering that PBS consisted of very creative-type people, we decided to also try to be creative. We prepared a proposal using caricatures of the personnel to be assigned. Of course, this meant that the pictures we used would show me as the only black surrounded by whites. The leader of the office's audit practice felt uncomfortable with this approach. However, we went ahead with the plan which proved successful. PBS said that one of the reasons we were selected was that we showed creativity and were not afraid to take a stand that might be considered by some as controversial.

After the PBS triumph, we began winning several other major clients—major associations, colleges and other nonprofits. One of the reasons for our success was the ability to listen to clients, learn their true needs and then show them how our services could help them meet their needs.

Too often, people don't really listen to each other. They are too set in their opinions and on convincing others that they are correct. In doing so, they often miss out on truly understanding what others are saying.

I worked hard to strengthen our relationship with Howard University, which was in trouble. By the end of my first year, we had issued our audit report covering the current year as well as all back years.

In the meantime, I also realized the opportunities that existed in providing services to the District of Columbia government. Steve advised me that local politics was a huge part of what the company was about in D.C. He proved invaluable to this second phase of my career. He had helped convince me to come to D.C. in the first place, and he introduced me around to all the important people I needed to know and gave me a lot of freedom.

I respected Steve, but I never liked politics and had no plans of making it a part of my daily life. I understood, however, that in a place like D.C. it was hard for a black executive for a major accounting firm to remain outside the political fray. For the most part, I was able to do just that.

While D.C. afforded me my highest level of success with Peat Marwick, it was also by far the lowest point in my career. During this time, the firm lost the Howard University account—during a change of the university's president and its chief financial officer in 1986. We would resume the account in 1991 with the arrival of another new president and another new CFO.

In 1986, Howard University was changing presidents for the first time in 20-plus years. By that time, Peat Marwick had been involved with the school for a long time, but always with the understanding that a change at the helm could be a risk for us.

Howard was struggling with a problem with its financial aid process. Peat Marwick was brought in during the middle of the year to straighten out the situation. We were not only able to fix the problem but also able to secure $20 million in financial aid. We set up a new financial system within three months time. It had been a job well done and one that at any other time would have definitely put us on the radar screen in a positive way. This was short lived.

We found ourselves embroiled in academic politics. Dr. Franklyn G. Jenifer, the newly elected president of Howard, also had a new CFO—one that I had actually referred to the school. In the end, however, the CFO refused to acknowledge the role I had played in securing his job and actually gave someone else the credit. The CFO started a campaign to discredit Peat Marwick, and we soon discovered he wanted to bring in another firm.

Richard D. Parsons—the current chairman and CEO of Times Warner Inc.—chaired Howard University's auditing committee at the time. I met with Richard to discuss our problem. Unfortunately, while he understood the political ramifications of the decision, he let me know there was nothing that could be done. He made it very clear to me that they had just hired a new president and therefore they had to support his decisions. Nevertheless, when the president notified me they were changing auditors, I was stunned, hurt and emotionally dismayed.

Although I felt that this last incident had an impact on my career, I stayed focused on meeting the needs of my other clients and continued to gain new clients to make up for the lost revenue. In truth, I was vividly aware that the loss of such a large client would likely be a mar on my career record.

Dr. Milton Wilson, former dean of Howard's business school, had asked me to teach auditing courses at the university back in 1981, and I had continued to do so until this incident. After the president's disturbing decision, however, I found that I simply could not continue to teach at Howard. I took what I would later call an informal sabbatical, but I returned at the end of the year.

After the second year, I'd gotten past my slump, and during the next five years I worked hard to reposition the office. By the time we resumed working with Howard, we had either recruited or were in the process of recruiting numerous other large clients. These included such nonprofit organizations as the American Red Cross, National Geographic, the American Association of Retired Persons (AARP) and Smithsonian Institution.

We had begun to work with all the major universities in the area—Georgetown University, George Washington University, Gallaudet University and Catholic University of America. We had also built a very successful federal audit practice.

From time to time, I was forced to make appearances at local political events. As Steve constantly pointed out to me, much of our work came from the city government; and the political leaders were the people who could help make that happen.

During my 25-year tenure with the firm in D.C., I worked directly or indirectly with three different D.C. mayors—Marion S. Barry, Sharon Pratt Kelly and Anthony A. Williams. While I never ran in the mayors' circles, I got to know each of their key people very well and gained their respect.

Steve never let up, though, telling me I should develop a closer relationship with the mayors. I think he finally realized that I was too set in my ways to change my approach this late in my life. Yet, while the political lifestyle was not one I was interested in, I learned to keep ties to political insiders without compromising my position about politics.

Elijah Rogers, a well-respected official in Mayor Barry's administration, gave me some of the best advice of my career. He said: "Don't pay attention to me or the mayor—pay attention to the young, up-and-coming folk in the government. They're the ones who will be in a position to help you down the road."

He gave me the names of three young people working in the city government. I had good common sense enough to follow Elijah's advice and to cultivate great relationships with each of these young people. All three advanced to top officials in city government and subsequently outside of government. They have been invaluable to me over the years.

I have always relied on my common sense. Because I was a partner in the country's largest international accounting firm, top officials in D.C. city government opened their doors to me and answered my phone calls.

When the young officials became the city's power brokers, they remembered me.

I met Tony Williams when he was CFO for the District of Columbia. When he told me he was considering running for mayor, I advised against it. Of course, he didn't listen to me, and I guess that proves that my common sense is outside the realm of politics.

My years in D.C. have been full of new lessons and challenges. Since that point in my career when I was sure D.C. wasn't the place for me, I've learned what strength it takes to test myself. I became a better person and a better manager in the process. There were parts of my job I learned to enjoy such as business development, relationship building and problem solving.

There are also things that come natural to me that I learned were invaluable to my career such as good listening skills; an innate sense of timing, which gave me a knack for tailoring the clients' needs with the needs of the company; and my love for community development and working to make our communities better. These skills proved invaluable as I progressed as a partner.

Young professionals often think that to be a successful partner you have to develop new business. This scares many of them off, and they begin to look for other career paths. What they need to focus on are the skills around their technical abilities, problem-solving, team-building and their listening skills. By developing these skills they can become a successful partner. Doors will open, and new opportunities will come their way.

One of the most satisfying aspects of this period was enjoying the success the Washington office was experiencing. We were achieving success in becoming the auditors of major nonprofits but also seeing other people—especially Rich and Kathy McKinless, who were now the partners in charge of our nonprofit practice—succeeding in winning these large engagements.

Another satisfying area was building a strong audit practice that also provided services to the federal government. KPMG had a strong federal consulting practice over the years, but it was very difficult to transfer our reputation to the federal government audit area.

As I became partner in charge of the Washington office audit practice and the managing partner, we began to gain momentum in building this practice through the efforts of younger partners who I was instrumental in bringing into the practice. John Hummel, who led this practice, and Diane Dudley, who worked with him, were critical to the success of our office. It ultimately became the model practice for providing audit services to the federal government.

17

IT TAKES A VILLAGE: MENTORS IN MY PERSONAL AND PUBLIC LIFE

My life has been positively touched by so many people that it would be futile to try and single out any few. I am who I am because of the people who early on instilled in me the values and sense of self that would sustain me throughout my life. There were people I met along my journey who—for one reason or another—took an interest in my success and took time from their own personal lives to help me.

The lists of guides, advisers, guardians and mentors were many. They included my mother, Ruby; my father, Reginald (in spirit and through his DNA); my indefatigable Uncle and memorable Auntie; and my brothers who were the closest to soul mates I'd ever have. Also, I can't forget the many neighbors who warily watched my growth and stumbles, pushing me along even when I didn't want them to; and friends; bosses; religious advisers; and business colleagues. Certainly my immediate family: Cecelia, the love of my life and my alter ego; and Michelle and Michael, the most wonderful children any man could hope to have.

There are a number of people whose faces or names come automatically to mind when someone out of the blue asks, "Who would you say has influenced your life the most?" Because there's not enough room here to list all the contributors to my life, I have listed just a few people whose contributions have greatly affected my life. These are people who, had they not been present during my journey, I am certain the journey would not have played out as successfully and miraculously as it did.

The fact that my father is on this list befuddles most people who know me. My family, friends and close colleagues know that I was just 9 months old when my father passed away. So, while I have no personal recollection of Reginald Ross, what I have learned from relatives and family members convinces me that I have inherited a great deal from him. And what I have learned from my spiritual journey is that his spirit lives on and has always been a guide for me.

My love for business as well as my knack for approaching business from a common sense perspective, I am told, comes from my father. My sincere respect for people who work with or for me and my gaining their respect in return is something most family members tell me was one of my father's most memorable attributes. I was told early on that he was viewed as a benevolent businessman, and that is what I have tried throughout my career to shape myself into.

The inherent traits could not have been learned in textbooks. Neither could the best of instructors have passed them on during classroom sessions. I would not have picked up the innate traits I share with my father from any other person or document—and there is no other explanation for my ability to handle situations or resolve issues one way rather than another, except his being with me in spirit.

My St. Kitts relatives describe something called the "Ross ways" that each of my siblings and I share. Gratefully, I was able to build on what comes absolutely natural to me, combine it with my theoretical and book learning and become a better person. The same skills that made my father the successful estate manager he was have been invaluable to my own career path. I think his entrepreneurialism is in my blood. Somewhere in my subconscious I think I wanted to emulate him in my adult life.

My sense is that my mother was every bit as phenomenal as my father. She was, by all reports, a special human being. What I have realized more as I grow older is that Ruby Ross shaped my life more than anyone else ever could. Her strong commitment to keep us together rather than separate us was a great sacrifice for her; and nothing I have achieved in my life would have been possible had she not made that sacrifice.

Some scientists believe it is a mother's innate bonding with her children that gives her a special wisdom. My mother surely foresaw that the four of us would need each other in life, whether we remained in St. Kitts or traveled to America. As the youngest child, my mother's commitment to me was especially important because in St. Kitts' culture, the youngest child would not have been the one relatives would willingly choose to take in as their own.

When we moved to the United States, God again must have been watching over us when we ended up in the close-knit community of Runyon Heights. While former first lady Hillary Rodham Clinton is credited for coining the adage, "It takes a village to raise a child," that theory was alive and well in Runyon Heights in the 1950s when I was growing up there.

Runyon Heights and our church, Metropolitan A.M.E. Zion Church, were parts of the village that helped raise my brothers and me. The adults in our community saw our future as part of each of their responsibilities. I cannot say who or what I would have been had I not been raised in that kind of environment, but I can say without reservation that much of who I am can be attributed to the many mothers and fathers who believed it was their responsibility to help raise a responsible and productive child.

Growing up in Yonkers, I cannot point to any instance of overt racism, but now I know there were plenty of instances of subtle racism. It was part of the fabric of the city. We learned how to deal with the subtleties of racism—people didn't want you to be certain places, to compete with them in certain ways. They didn't have to say anything; we learned to recognize it quite early.

This community of retired laborers and housekeepers in Runyon Heights convinced me that I could achieve anything. And though we were far from rich, they made us know we had everything we needed to lead a successful life. Few of these voluntary caretakers were formally educated or held professional titles, but most had incredible wisdom about life that must have been the result of their own experiences. Their advice and counsel were in hopes that we didn't experience the same obstacles they had. That was worth so much more than any amount of money could have bought.

J.B. Johnson, one of the adult members of Metropolitan church, probably never knew the impact he had on my childhood—the wonderful memories I still hold dear. While my uncle, probably because of his injury, didn't spend time with me or my brothers outside the home, Mr. Johnson took me to my first baseball game at Yankee Stadium and to my first circus at Madison Square Garden. For a child, these were enormously invaluable gifts. I still remember his station wagon.

Uncle and Auntie were critical to my life and my success, as well as to my brothers'. From the time we arrived in America, they became our American guardians. That relationship became even more critical less than a year after our arrival, when my mother returned to St. Kitts. Thanks to these new parents, my brothers and I were raised in a caring, supportive environment and given the opportunity to pursue the American dream. They also gave us a value system that stayed with me throughout my life. They made personal sacrifices that, to this date, I'm not sure I would've made if I were in their shoes.

While Uncle didn't have financial wealth, he taught us the basics and passed on to us the values we would need to be successful in this unwelcoming world: a strong work ethic, perseverance, the ability to dream impossible dreams and the self-confidence to pursue those dreams. He taught us to ignore the obstacles, to move forward and never look back with regret. He had a lot to do with the mental focus we developed over the years.

So much of what I have accomplished over the years, I attribute to Uncle. He didn't teach me how to be sensitive or any of that touchy-feely stuff, but I learned a sense of myself—a pride in who I am.

As children, when we listened to his endless stories of his own harsh life and how he never let any obstacles stop him from doing what he wanted, we would shake our heads or roll our eyes—waiting for the moment he would finish. I cannot tell you how many times we heard the story of his 20-mile treks to his job as a carpenter!

Beyond my family and community, there were others who touched my life in irrevocable ways—people like Emsar Bradford, the first black CPA I ever met. He was my first role model in the accounting field, and he taught me a number of life lessons that would stay with me. More than anything, he showed me what was possible, in spite of the odds.

During the 38 years I worked at Peat Marwick, which merged with Klynveld Main Goerdeler in 1987 to form KPMG, I had the pleasure of working with some of the best accounting professionals in the world. Many of these men became friends after they were mentors, and each of them played critical roles in the support and counsel I needed during my journey.

There are many KPMG associates and colleagues who helped make my career with the firm an incredible ride. There are a handful of people—including some I've mentioned previously such as Jim Powers, Steve Harlan and Sy Bohrer—who I can truthfully say that without their mentorship during various points of my career, it would have been a far more difficult journey and one that quite possibly would have turned out less stellar.

Tony Natelli was the managing partner of the Washington office when I first met him between 1968 and 1970. Tony was born in New Jersey to Italian parents and was on a fast rise within the firm. He had just returned from being the managing partner of the Rome office, and most people in the company thought he might someday be chairman of the firm.

I was only a young supervising senior accountant in the New York office when Tony asked me to come to Washington to help the firm recruit at Howard University which was a major source of black recruits as well as a major client of the Washington office. During those visits, Tony and I would get into discussions about racism, and I would make every attempt to explain to him some of the problems black recruits would face as they joined the firm.

Tony would always listen very carefully and then tell me that I should understand that racism was not limited to blacks. He explained how he had faced racism as an Italian American. These discussions helped me gain a much broader understanding of racism in America. Most importantly, it gave me self-confidence that a managing partner would take the time to discuss these issues with me and treat me as a peer.

Tony left the firm shortly after that and ultimately became one of the most successful real estate developers in the Greater Washington area. Throughout the years we remained friends. When I moved to the Washington office and advanced to managing partner, I knew I could always count on Tony for help and support.

He sponsored my son's peewee football team and supported many community organizations I was involved in when they needed financial help. He also gave my son his first summer job as a construction worker between high school and college.

I cannot talk about mentors without mentioning my wife. We often don't think of our spouses as mentors. But Cecelia was very supportive to me in my career and all the related areas, including education, church and community. She was always there to help me confront my fears, irritations, angers or concerns. She was a patient listener and a good adviser. She has been and continues to be an important "co-worker" in all aspects of my life.

PART V

THE NATIONAL ASSOCIATION OF BLACK ACCOUNTANTS

18

THE BIRTH OF NABA

In a perfect world, the rule of one would no longer exist in America's accounting industry. It was 40 years ago when I started at Peat Marwick and experienced what being the first and only really means. When I was hired, it was daunting to be the second black picked by one of the top accounting firms in America. I was the only professional black employed in the New York office.

When I became a CPA in 1969, there had only been approximately 125 black CPAs in the country, compared to more than 100,000 CPAs overall. As late as 1977, when I became a partner, there were over 5,000 partners in the major accounting firms in the country, but only about five were black.

So, along with this pride and excitement of being courted and picked by a Big Eight firm came a litany of other emotions that accompanied those feelings. My self-confidence was real, but others' confidence in me had to be earned over and over again. I was also weighted down with the knowledge that my every move was under a microscope—that I was carrying the weight of the black race on my shoulders. I had the double fear of being new on the job and being black. Would I fit in? Would I be accepted?

I understood the white environment and had had extensive experience being one of a few blacks in a sea of white faces from high school to college. But that wasn't enough to prepare me for the day-to-day experience of working beside whites—many of whom felt I threatened their own space and position.

Competition was nothing new to me. I have always thrived on competition and had competed with the brightest and best in high school and college. But this, again, was different. There was no one who looked like me to validate me; no one with whom I felt comfortable discussing my concerns and fears; no one there who understood exactly what I was going through.

While skills and capability are the most important attributes any employee must bring to his or her new company, almost as important for a successful career are strong mentors and a supportive and nuturing network. With mentorships and nuturing networks, young black professionals going into public accounting are much less likely to experience the loneliness that most early entrants experienced during the early days of affirmative action and civil rights laws.

In the years I worked in public accounting, I had more than my share of opportunities to experience firsthand the ugliness of racism, stereotyping and prejudice within the corporate environment. I have also experienced the limitations placed on me because I had to prove myself over and over again. My blessing was that I had great mentors through-out my career. Although they were white, they somehow understood that I had what it took to be good at what I did . . . if given the opportunity. Sadly, every young black accountant that walks through those pristine doors won't be so lucky.

But even these conscientious mentors had their own cultural limitations. There were concerns I had that there was no way they could understand or empathize with. And even if they wanted to, they couldn't protect me from all the negatives existing within those corridors of power. Because of this, even as we celebrate the growing number of young black professionals entering the accounting industry and advancing into the partnership of these firms and even into leadership positions, there is and always will be the need for another level of support—mentors, technical advisers, counselors and networking for those coming into the field.

Although the number of blacks who have achieved success in public accounting is still very small, the numbers succeeding to the partner level and to senior partner positions in these firms are increasing. These partners have major responsibilities to mentor younger blacks as well as others. They cannot forget that someone mentored them and that because of this they were in a position to succeed.

There were many other people who contributed to my ability to work in the mostly white environment for 38 years. For me, it made all the difference in the world that there was a Caspa Harris before me at Peat Marwick. He was the first black hired by the firm. Ironically, Caspa was CFO at Howard University when I first transferred to the Washington office.

Caspa was a friend, a sounding board, as well as a client; and he understood the concerns and challenges I was facing at the firm. I shared my concerns with him. Something seemingly as simple as having someone to discuss this with helped tremendously. Our friendship was very important during that time in my career.

Don't let anyone fool you, being apart of a group or a network gives you an emotional edge that you don't have when you're the first or the only. One of the ways I handled this isolation was to stay connected with my old church and community. This, too, helped me remain grounded as I advanced in my career. I recommend to every young professional to find some vehicle to help stay grounded as you advance in your career. This could be the church you grew up in, your fraternity or sorority, or organizations such as the National Association of Black Accountants (NABA).

19

NABA: Starting From Ground Zero

The National Association of Black Accountants was created in my living room in Bronx, New York. That meeting was in response to the city of New York's 1968 civil rights lawsuit against six of the Big Eight accounting firms headquartered in New York City seeking the hiring of more blacks. Arthur Andersen and Ernst & Ernst were headquartered in Chicago and Cleveland, respectively, and therefore were not included in the lawsuit.

Our first meeting in December 1969 included about 16 black New York accountants. But the number quickly dwindled down to the "NABA Nine"—the nine who would become recognized by NABA as its founding members: Ronald Benjamin, Earl Biggot, Donald Bristow, Kenneth Drummond, Bertram Gibson, Richard McNamee, George Wallace, Michael Winston and me.

Our monthly meetings centered on what we perceived as a half-step effort by the firms to hire young, black accountants but not prepare them for success. We saw this as setting them up for failure. On the other end of the spectrum, there was a great deal of discussion about whether our group would be perceived as a political threat and whether it would be accepted by the Big Eight accounting firms and black CPAs, as well as the profession as a whole.

The general consensus was that the organization was not a "black power" political group since we all knew that whites, especially corporate and accounting-type industries, associated this term with violence or militancy. There would later be consternation about naming the organization "black," again with the reservation of offending the white establishment. That concern was disregarded as we moved forward. In the end, there were many more people interested in forming such a group, but some of them were afraid to "rock the boat" or stir up the ire of those companies that were already offering jobs to a few black accountants.

The issue at hand for those of us who felt strongly enough to continue was the need for change in the recruitment and retention of blacks coming into the accounting industry. We realized that if any changes were forthcoming, we would need to be at least the precipitator of those changes.

Bert Mitchell, in a 1969 article published in the *Journal of Accountancy,* challenged the accounting industry by publicizing the gap between black accountants and others in the field. Based on his Ford Foundation-funded survey of 52 accounting firms, there were 150 black CPAs out of a total of 100,000 accountants. The employment records for most of these firms, he found, were dismal. At that point, no blacks had been made partner at a firm, although there were 3,139 partners at the 52 firms surveyed.

Mitchell pointed out that even though the medical profession required more rigor and preparation, "the proportion of blacks in medicine was almost 14 times as much as in professional accounting." His study conceded that there were some firms that recognized the need to increase their intake and promotion of blacks in the field, but their steps toward doing so were remedial, at best.

On the heels of Mitchell's findings, we became committed to establishing a networking vehicle for black accountants in the country. There weren't many of us at that time—approximately 30 working at major New York City accounting firms. Amazingly, less than five years earlier, the major accounting firms had been virtually segregated.

Our first challenge was to identify the different black accountants that NABA would eventually represent. Some accountants were employed in public accounting and some had their own practices. Others were employed by corporate firms or government agencies. There were certified accountants, but most were just accountants.

Our second challenge was to communicate to experienced black CPAs the need for an organization that would represent blacks and encourage increased involvement in the accounting profession and solicit support for our efforts from the accounting industry. Unfortunately, we were not very successful in gaining the trust that this organization would not be a lightning rod for the accounting firms many of these potential candidates now worked for or hoped to work for in the future. Many saw us as troublemakers who would create more problems than we would solve, or they were too busy trying to make it in their current work environments.

Our third major challenge was to gain acceptance by the Big Eight accounting firms, the American Institute of Certified Public Accountants (AICPA), the New York State Society (NYSS), as well as academia. NABA took some concrete steps to get across the message that there was a need for such an organization, that it would have a positive impact on the accounting profession, and that it was not some type of black militant organization. In light of the political environment of the 1960s, this was not a simple task. Established black accountants were some of our harshest and most vocal critics.

Our first big event was a panel discussion with representatives from AICPA, NYSS, the Big Eight accounting firms and black CPAs. This function was held at the Old Biltmore Hotel near Grand Central Station in New York.

Dr. Sybil C. Mobley, legendary dean of the Florida A&M University School of Business, participated in one of the panels. At that time, Dr. Mobley was accounting department chair at FAMU. Most of the large accounting firms sent representatives from their executive offices to this meeting. I'm sure most of them came to make sure we weren't planning anything radical. From all accounts, this was a very successful meeting, and it was here that we gained acceptance.

Those who were members of the AICPA and the NYSS committees on minority recruitment would not support us when we made presentations about NABA and its needs. They were the ones who questioned why such an organization was needed. At other times we would meet on a one-on-one basis with established black accountants. They would listen to us but politely dismiss us and this idea of NABA as something that wasn't needed.

It was also at this initial meeting that we laid out the goals of the organization:

1. To assist and encourage members of minority groups in their effort to enter the accounting profession;

2. To stimulate acquaintance and fellowship among members of minority groups;

3. To provide opportunities for members of minority groups to increase their knowledge of accounting and to increase their individual capabilities; and

4. To unite, through membership in the association, people interested in enhancing opportunities in accounting for members of minority groups.

This meeting was a big step in opening up dialogue and gaining acceptance of NABA by the accounting industry. There were both discomfort and distrust between industry management and blacks being brought into these firms.

Both parties had to get past the fact that the Big Eight firms had only begun opening their doors to blacks in a meaningful manner after a New York City lawsuit was filed. While the industry's idea of opening doors was minimal and very selective, NABA hoped to make it easier to push the door even wider—increasing opportunities, retention and upward mobility for blacks who walked through.

Most of the firms' hiring activities were blatant knee-jerk reactions to the lawsuit. They identified and hired a small number of African-American accountants—mostly recruited from the predominantly black colleges in the South—and offered little in the way of assistance to help the young accountants adjust to their new environments. They made no allowances for the new hires who came from predominantly black colleges or universities in the South and had no orientation to big city life.

White managers felt that students from the black colleges were not as well prepared or as smart as the students from white colleges.

It is interesting to note that several of the early black hires left the major firms to successfully pursue their MBA degrees from such colleges as Harvard University, Wharton College and others.

Most likely, some firms brought new hires into the big New York offices with full knowledge that the new employees would suffer readjustment problems and oftentimes require a longer orientation period than some of their other employees. In spite of this common sense knowledge, the new hires received less than adequate training in some offices and little or no training in others. The unspoken and sometimes spoken attitude was that most blacks simply could not cut it in the public accounting field. This attitude fed into the high and constant turnover rate of black employees at these firms.

The complaint was that black accountants were losing accounts with great potential. But the employees' retort was that they had little direction and no assistance from their managers. The most important piece missing in that paradigm was the lack of a network and mentors. Even with a very strong academic foundation, you must have a network, a support system and mentors to guide you and help you avoid the obvious traps. Without this level of support and foundation, it's very, very difficult for a young black accountant to make it in this competitive arena.

Some would say that many of the issues blacks faced in the late 1960s no longer exist. Many would disagree.

One former accountant with one of the largest accounting firms in the country resigned in 1999 and submitted a resignation letter that spelled out his dismay with that particular firm's promotion practices and his own experiences during his six years with the firm.

Without a doubt, the employee's experiences mirrored that of hundreds of, if not most, minority accountants who found themselves working in the consistently white, male-dominated ivory towers.

Upon joining the firm in 1993, the employee informed his manager of his deep interest in working with international clients, given the fact that his parents had emigrated from another country. Fortunately, he was signed up for this group and placed as an entry-level staff member. After spending two years as a staff member on one major international engagement, however, he was pulled from working with the client and told that due to his lack of experience, he would be replaced with an employee who had more experience and knowledge in the industry. A month later, he learned that his replacement was not only at his level but also had no more specialized experience than he had.

According to the resignation letter, the frustrated employee said he "thought this was simply a part of how the business worked, until it happened again." He learned quickly that although he was viewed as "good enough" to be a staff person on the engagements, he was not good enough to "run" the engagements.

His frustration grew as he watched other employees being transferred from different offices at levels comparable or lower than his level. The others were nurtured and given opportunities to work on public clients within his specified industry. Eventually, his client base was filtered out, leaving few engagements other than the not-for-profit clientele. To make matters worse, his managers consistently questioned his loyalty, saying he only performed up to par when he was working with clients he liked.

In the letter, the employee said his decision to leave the accounting firm came when he received a call from a human resources officer asking if he would be interested in a position as assistant to the recruiting director. In essence, he was being offered a demotion and reduction in responsibilities. Obviously, his effort to take charge of his career—as his manager often told him—was not working within the environment, neither was his efforts to identify a mentor. "Not having the groundwork others had to work with or the mentorship, I was destined to perform below par," he said.

Ironically, the employee was consistently called upon to teach experienced managers, to act in the capacity of both senior manager and manager for the busy seasons on certain clients and to teach the entire practice office the new internal control approach.

The fact is that most partners of that accounting firm had SEC experience, and most had close relationships with "key" people within their practice office. They all had excellent mentoring relationships with seniors who supported them 100 percent.

In his resignation letter, the employee made suggestions to the firm for correcting some of the innate problems that led to his difficult work experience as a minority in the corporate accounting environment:

> 1. "Ensure that the mentoring process for minorities is bolstered by action and not simply talk of action. Minorities in the practice office have no one to turn to when they have concerns. They need someone who will represent them 100 percent within the practice offices.

2. "The client assignment process needs to look at why minorities (especially people of African descent) are assigned to not-for-profit clients. Many of the minorities want the opportunity to work on challenging assignments in high-profile industries such as high-tech and other major public companies. However, they are routinely placed with less visible and less challenging clients.

3. "The evaluation process needs to be more timely, candid and fair. Many minorities believe the evaluation process is unfair and that they are being judged more harshly than their peers."

NABA moved from its infancy where meetings were held in members' homes—sometimes around the dinner table as we ate and talked and discussed strategies—to full acceptance as a national organization by 1970. The nine founders decided we had discussed what had to be done long enough and agreed to certify the organization. It was officially incorporated that year.

Our first thought was to use the organization to help new accountants improve their technical skills. But NABA gradually took on its own life, eventually growing from nine members in 1969 into a national organization with more than 5,000 members in more than 100 cities today.

These members represent accounting professionals as well as students aiming for careers in accounting in more than 50 professional chapters and 100 student chapters in 27 states and the District of Columbia.

As in most organizations, there were some growing pains involved in the shaping and expansion of NABA. Some of the new members came in with their own agendas; others believed they better understood what the black accounting community needed. To a great extent, it became a battleground for accountants seeking power and their own constituency.

I served as president of NABA in 1969 and 1970. In 1971, I knew it was time for me to refocus my energies. There was another group actively campaigning to take over leadership of NABA, and one of the founders, Ken Drummond, asked me to run again. While I did run again, my heart wasn't in it, and I lost to my opponent by one vote.

It was during this time that I realized just how overextended I was. My wife was complaining that I didn't spend enough time at home, especially with our daughter; and a partner at Peat Marwick, not knowing about my involvement with NABA, questioned my commitment to the company.

Much of NABA's success came from the fact that both whites and blacks viewed the founders and my early leadership in the organization as positive signs that it was a serious organization. They viewed my role as assurance that it was not a radical organization out to go against the system.

In spite of inner conflicts through the years and an effort to revamp—and even discredit the early founders of the organization—NABA continues to be a great organization serving new and veteran accountants throughout the country. It has been at the forefront of developing programs and possible solutions to problems involving the recruitment and retention of blacks in the accounting field.

Over the first 30 plus years, NABA established an annual convention that drew more than 1,000 professionals and 100 student members, as well as 300 corporate representatives. The national scholarship program has awarded more than $6 million in its 30 years of existence.

The annual convention consisted of technical sessions, seminars, career fairs and networking activities. There were also four annual regional student conferences—offering seminars and interviews for permanent accounting positions—that brought approximately 1,200 students and 200 corporate representatives together. A minority accountant recruitment service and job placement service match professional minority accountants with potential employers.

While these programs have made a significant difference in the number of students going into public accounting and those being promoted within the firms, there is still a huge gap between the growth in black accountants in the public firms and overall growth.

Possibly because of my affiliation with NABA, one of my first assignments as a new partner in the New York office was to research and complete a one-year study on the concerns of minority employees that resulted in the firm's poor retention record of black employees. The final report was shared with Peat Marwick leadership in hopes of implementing programs and directives that would increase retention rates of black employees and to do a better job of recruiting outstanding black graduates.

My report included candid conversations with 118 black Peat Marwick professionals in 39 operating offices, 12 Peat Marwick alumni, and partners and managers in 10 operating offices. I also had an opportunity to meet with both current and former employees of the other seven major accounting firms. In my talk with black professionals, I learned about specific problems, achievements and expectations from their careers. And from the alumni, I learned precisely why each had chosen to leave the firm and what their experiences had been since leaving.

In my final report, one of the points I made was that the problems weren't just with Peat Marwick, but were industrywide—centering on recruiting and maintaining quality black accounting personnel. But because Peat Marwick was the largest accounting firm in the country at that time, it was my opinion that the firm should be the leader in the recruitment and retention of black accounting professionals.

To upper management's amazement, the study revealed findings that ran counter to what the industry had long believed or accepted as fact, such as:

- It was long believed that the majority of black professionals were graduates of predominantly black schools—hence were less likely to succeed within the firm. In fact, only 20 percent of the black professionals employed by the firm graduated from black colleges, and 28 percent of those held advanced degrees from leading graduate schools.

- Three of five black audit managers and supervisors were graduates of black colleges.

- A majority of the black professionals I talked with perceived career opportunities as "fair" or "poor."

- Black professionals encountered greater difficulty in being accepted by their supervisors and their peers than they encountered in being accepted by clients.

- Of 54 blacks employed for more than one year, only nine acknowledged having had a mentor at work, and in only a few instances was this mentor a member of management.

To this date, I strongly believe that many of the problems currently encountered by black professionals are common problems shared by all within the industry. They relate to client assignments, on-the-job training, performance evaluation, advancement and compensation. Because of factors unique to minorities, these common problems became crucial to a minority's perception of his or her career opportunities with the firm and, in many instances, become the proverbial "final straw" that caused them to leave at the first opportunity.

But the work of NABA is far from done. In many respects, many of the problems we focused on in the 1970s continue today. Low numbers of blacks being recruited into the profession, lack of upward mobility, low retention, and the problem of new accountants learning how to deal with the subtle racism and prejudices are still prevalent in the accounting field.

The concerns identified in the 1977 study continued to be reported into the next decades by new and younger professional employees. While the good news for the accounting industry was that more blacks and minorities were being given opportunities to walk through the doors, the bad news was that more young, black professionals were experiencing lack of upward mobility, low retention and the problem of having to learn to recognize and work around the subtle biases inherent in a workplace that has been traditionally whites only. New hires were still complaining of job isolation, stagnation in their jobs and lack of mentorships within their organizations.

It is interesting to note that the result of a recent study by Howard University's Center for Accounting Education shows that very little has changed. One study surveyed black employees of the major accounting firms, while the second study interviewed NABA members. The second study found:

- 63.7 percent of the respondents feel no obligation to remain with their current organization.

- 58.5 percent of the respondants feel that the mistakes they make in the workplace affect the evaluation of other members in their racial group.

- 49.2 percent believe that their white counterparts with less technical competence or experience have been given more high profile/challenging job assignments.

- 55 percent believe that because of their race, they have not always received unbiased/objective evaluations from their white supervisors.

Free-lance writer Phaedra Brotherton chronicled the progress and stagnancies of blacks in accounting in an article in the October 2005 issue of the *Journal of Accountancy.*

The article, entitled "A History of Determination: Minority CPAs Have Come a Long Way, But True Diversity Has Yet to Be Achieved," pointed out that civil rights efforts impacting black accountants began as far back as the mid-1940s, when President Franklin D. Roosevelt's New Deal barred discrimination in federal government and federal contractor employment. Yet, it said blacks remain under-represented at large CPA firms.

Jesse B. Blayton, who is known as the "dean of Negro accountants," was one of America's earliest black CPAs and Georgia's first. He is credited with inspiring generations of black CPAs. He became a Morehouse College professor, helping to establish the school's business department, and later served as chairman of Atlanta University's accounting department. He was also one of a small group of blacks invited to meet with President Roosevelt's advisers to discuss the president's New Deal initiative from an African-American perspective.

Brotherton said the passage of the 1964 Civil Rights Act, with the creation of the Equal Employment Opportunity Commission, was the real turning point for black accountants. In the late 1960s, the AICPA founded the Committee on Recruitment for Minority Groups, and in 1969 the *Journal of Accountancy* published an article entitled, "The Black Minority in the CPA Profession." The article showed the dismal ratio of blacks in the accounting profession—a total of 150 black CPAs compared to 100,000 accountants in the country.

With the onset of the Civil Rights Act and a nationally spotlighted lawsuit by the city of New York, accounting firms began an abbreviated effort to recruit at historically black colleges and universities. While they hired some young black accounting graduates into their organizations, this opened up another can of worms for the schools. Not only would the accounting firms deem many of the graduates unprepared for accounting work, but the Association of Advanced Collegiate Schools of Business (AACSB) also required that most of the schools' faculty have either a PhD, or in the case of the accounting teachers, a combination of a CPA certificate and an MBA. Many HBCUs did not meet these criteria in the 1960s.

The AICPA committee on minority recruitment, under the leadership of director Sharon Donahue, geared two early programs toward helping HBCUs increase the number of CPAs and PhDs on their faculties. It offered a scholarship program for instructors on an interim basis so they could pursue PhDs; summer seminars that focused on building teaching skills; and CPE credits for the instructors.

When NABA was founded, its initial purpose was to provide networking opportunities, professional development and support for young black accountants coming into public accounting firms. In that same era, the National Association of Minority CPA Firms was started with a grant from the Nixon administration's office of minority affairs.

Women, Asian and Latino groups also formed their own associations for much the same purposes—to network and build mentoring relationships.

Brotherton concluded that while much progress had been made in the accounting arena for minority groups, the percentage of minority CPAs still remains low. One of the most recent statistics shows that only 7 percent of CPAs employed by accounting firms are minorities.

Mentors, she pointed out, are a key component of success in the large accounting firms. Since the days of Jesse Blayton, accounting faculty members have served as mentors for minority CPAs.

George S. Willie, partner at Bert Smith & Co., said: "Educators have to be an integral part of our efforts. There has to be an intensified outreach program to academia. The families of minority students must promote commerce, accounting and finance as alternatives to the ministry, medicine and law. Equally critical is the involvement of mature and accomplished finance and accounting professionals. Professionals of ethnic minorities are clear evidence that with hard work, the right relationships and the proper focus, there is much to be attained in the accounting profession."

While some people can say I "made it," the best part of being accepted as a leader in my field is that the decision makers will listen to me when I bend their ear about what they should be doing to recruit and retain good accountants who happen to be minority.

I feel a deep responsibility because of my achievements for making sure that five or 10 years from now there will be many more of us who have "made it." That number should be increasing exponentially. I was elected as the first president of NABA, and now I'm the most senior active member. What that tells me is that we have been doing something right.

I am proud and often amazed at what came out of nine black accountants' early dreams of making things better and easier for young professionals coming after us—of hopefully opening the doors a little wider for them to walk through.

NABA is now recognized as the voice of the black accountant. It is the only association that seeks to make Dr. King's dream a reality in the accounting profession. In 1984, the AICPA Future Issues Committee made a statement when it did not include the role of minorities as one of the 14 major issues facing the profession. In not considering the integration of the accounting profession one of its most pressing problems, the AICPA left a void into which NABA stepped and a leadership role that NABA is currently fulfilling.

NABA not only represents the black accountant working in public accounting, but it also now represents the black accountant in corporate America, the black accountant who owns his or her own business, the black accountant working in government and the black accounting educator. In short, it represents the interests of all black accountants. With this diverse membership base, NABA can influence policy and policy-makers. It is a strong and viable organization, one that the profession cannot afford to take lightly.

Among the many challenges of this 21st century, the accounting industry must face and deal with the problem of diversity and its willingness to hire and promote accountants of color. What will NABA's role be in this 21st century? It will be a test of what we have done for the last 30 plus years. It will be an opportunity for the new accounting leaders to open up the doors of the Big Four and other firms even further.

We have had 30 plus years of blacks working inside those ivory towers; and though you would think the rule of one or two or three might have disappeared, it's not so. We are not there yet, and we cannot stop or even rest until we are there. The pendulum keeps swinging.

While I'm not a political person by nature, I do understand that often it matters who is at the helm in the White House . . . and their philosophy on inclusion and opening up the doors dribble down to the private sector. Then you see progress. We have to be ready to take advantage of that when it happens and keep plugging away for change when it doesn't seem to be happening from on high. We also have to be aware that as the environment changes, politically, economically and socially, our method for addressing our concerns might require some change as well.

When we think of how important NABA is today, we also have to recognize the opportunities that membership provides. There are many. But, probably the most important is the opportunity for each member, young and old, to build a network of fellow professionals with shared experiences. This network provides mentoring opportunities and builds lifetime relationships that prove supportive during the most difficult times. It also offers business opportunities. I know that during my career, in every major city I could find a NABA professional who was able to introduce me to a potential contact when I needed such an introduction.

PART VI

ACHIEVING SUCCESS

20

LESSONS LEARNED

It's so very important that we learn about ourselves—our strengths and weaknesses. Each of us has our faults that can make a big difference in our career path.

When I feel strongly about something, there is nothing that can change my mind about it. Though my personality is one of balance, of staying pretty much on an even keel, my family is among the few people who know that I also have a temper that's virtually out of control once it's unleashed.

My first year at Peat Marwick, I worked on the United Artists account as assistant auditor. We often worked in the same room with the client's accounting staff. This meant that the client's staff would often hear everything being said by members of the engagement team. We had to always be careful of what we said.

One day, I was right in the middle of meeting with my client when this senior manager came over. He had a habit of coming into the room and loudly yelling negative statements or directions to me. This had been going on for quite some time, and I'd accepted it and ignored it as much as possible. But this was the day I would let him know how I felt. Once he'd gotten started, I stood up and let him know in no uncertain terms that I had had enough of his bullying and didn't appreciate his speaking to me that way, especially in front of the client's staff—the same people I was expected to get answers from.

He was smart enough to let me say those things; then he walked out. We met in the elevator later that day. He turned the elevator off and let me have it right there, saying I could be fired. I asked, "How do you expect me to gain respect from my clients when you walk in and degrade me in front of them?" He didn't really address that, but the point is, I had lost my temper and could very easily have lost my job.

Now that I know myself better and understand office politics better, I would certainly have talked to him alone, not in front of the whole room. At that instance, though, I didn't focus on what could happen after that. Ironically, my white clients told me afterward that they had been waiting for me to go after that manager. After that confrontation, I never in a million years would have expected to become a partner with the firm.

But I would never stop learning important lessons about myself and how to turn what others perceived as my weaknesses into strengths inside the corporate world. For instance, it took a while, but I eventually learned how to use my quiet demeanor—what some partners thought would be a detriment to my career path—to my advantage.

One reason why I seldom speak at meetings is that I noticed that in most meetings people paid little attention to what I was saying. Often someone else would repeat the same point I had made, and the rest of the group would agree with "his" great idea. Suddenly, my idea—the one I'd articulated earlier with no response—was suddenly a great idea and was being attributed to someone else.

I also noticed that some blacks would deal with this situation by being overly vocal. They would always have something to say or would constantly ask questions. Sometimes, they would raise their voices as they made a point. I realized that this was their way of making sure they were heard. Whenever I raised this point with the meeting leaders, I was constantly told that I was being overly sensitive and that it was not happening as I imagined.

After much deliberation about this problem, I decided to keep quiet, let everyone speak, observe what was being said. After a full discussion on the topic, I would summarize what was said and add my comments and suggestions in such a way that it would have been difficult to ignore.

More often, my suggestions became the basis of the solution to the problems that were discussed at the meeting.

Other Lessons that made my career path smoother . . .

1. I learned to ask questions early in my career rather than pretend I knew everything. For example, when I was assigned to the audit of cash under Joe Boyle, I understood fully how to reconcile bank accounts, but I had never dealt with the computerized bank reconciliation. After several days of floundering, Joe explained what I had to do in great detail. I quickly got on track and completed my assignment. I was over the budget by about 30 or 40 hours, but I learned from that experience to always ask questions when in doubt.

2. I learned to be confident in my technical abilities, even if others had a more technically advanced background.

3. I learned how important it was to make sure the entire team always moved in the same direction.

A strong and supportive team is not one where everyone always agrees. As a matter of fact, I valued teams that always pushed back the most. The key element that must exist is trust. You must be honest with the team members, and they will be honest with you. I always told them to tell me the problems first and after we deal with those problems, we can then discuss all the good, positive things. By doing this I always made certain that all the issues were placed on the table and no one was afraid to bring up the most difficult or embarrassing situation.

I also found that you need to support each of your team members even when they make mistakes. This helps to build trust. I always made sure that the team members were never afraid to try new ideas. This helps them grow and develop into a stronger team member.

I also realized that if I was going to be successful I could not let other people's biases take control. I had to take control of my career.

What I would learn after being a partner a few years was that most partners in those most coveted positions were to some extent "preselected" very early in their careers. There were silent or not-so-silent mentors helping these undeclared candidates climb up that ladder over the years. And by the time most of these men, and a few women, were announced as managing partner to lead an office at any of the largest firms in the country, they might be anywhere between 35 and 40 years old.

By 1983, I was 40 years old and hadn't received the sign that I was a preselected candidate for that ultimate ascension. I convinced myself that it might not ever happen and began my own quiet campaign, talking to key people in the firm, such as the area managing partner, or even the vice chairman when he visited the office, to let them know what and how I was feeling about my moving up in the firm. When I returned to the firm, I wanted to become managing partner in the firm some day. I doubt if I told anyone at the time about my desire other than maybe Jim Powers.

The question I asked was: "Do you think I can become a managing partner of the firm, and if so, which office would you consider transferring me to?" Each conversation ended with them confirming what I already believed—that I had the credentials and experience to become a managing partner. Most suggested that New York, Chicago, Los Angeles, Detroit or Washington would be good fits for me. But the conversation inevitably ended with this statement: "Frank, you're in just the right position to be ready for a move when one comes open . . . ."

By 1987, Joe Boyle was expected to become managing partner of our Washington office, when Steven Harlan was appointed vice chairman in charge of international. But instead they brought in Dave Fowler, who was partner in charge of human resources, and Joe remained partner in charge of the audit practice. When that happened, I saw the writing on the wall, and my hopes of ever making managing partner were virtually dashed. But I also commenced to do as I always had when I'm frustrated with a situation. I put my nose to the grindstone and kept doing my job to the best of my ability for the next three to four years.

When Dave Fowler retired in 1992, Joe Boyle became managing partner, and I became partner in charge of audits. Later that year, Joe suggested I put my name in the hat to become a member of the board. I did, and it turned out I was elected by my fellow partners to serve on the board, the highest policy-making body in KPMG.

Finally, I'm thankful for the support of all of my mentors over the years, but most of all I'm grateful for my self knowledge and the lessons I've learned. Because of this, I was able to take responsibility for my successes and failures, and in doing so I maintained control of my own destiny.

Although everyone will not fully agree with me, I believe that going to a predominantly white high school and college and at the same time living in a predominately black neighborhood taught me another important lesson that stayed with me throughout my entire career. That lesson is never let people know everything about you.

In short, I only let a few close friends and my immediate family know my true feelings. I found that whites are very forgiving of people from their own race but not always those of other races. During my early career, I remember one party where I saw partners and their wives "falling down" drunk. While I was watching, I noticed everyone thought it was funny. However, I realized that if it had been me, their reaction would've been very different—more critical of my behavior. I may have even been asked to leave the firm.

As I gained experience, I realized how important it was that I never allow anyone to place me in any of their stereotypical opinions of blacks. I could not dance, I wasn't loud nor did I wear flashy clothes, etc. Because of this my colleagues were forced to deal with me for who I was and not what they thought I should be.

———◆———

How did I balance my work and family life? If I'm to assume that I achieved any balance, it would be because of my wife's constant attempts at seeking a way to keep the family on an even keel.

Cecelia was always there for me. She attended to all the details that kept our house running smoothly. When the children were young, she was the balance between me and the kids. She did the carpooling, medical visits, shopping, cooking, playing and disciplining. Cecelia said raising the children was hard at times but always rewarding. However, she said that what kept her sane during those times were the immense support and babysitting help from both of our families.

Another thing that helped was the daily counseling sessions with lots of laughter from our neighbor and good friend Fran Krutchick. Fran and Bill Krutchick had children the same age as our children. Fran was especially helpful when Cecelia returned to school to get her degree in social work. Bill was also an accountant who worked for a local CPA firm.

I don't want to give the impression that I wasn't around at all. I was extremely busy keeping my career on track. There were a few nights of working all-nighters early on in my career. Cecelia started calling herself "the accounting widow." This was another time that Bill and Fran's friendship was helpful, as Bill was able to help her understand the demands of my working for a major public accounting firm.

Cecelia always found ways to get me involved in the kids' activities when it mattered. One of the things she found very helpful was my carpooling with other parents in the neighborhood to take the kids to religious education classes. She made sure that I attended all of my son's sports events. Vacations were taken every year even if it was only for a few days or a week. Daily family activities were carefully planned during these trips. There was to be no separate/individual interests.

Sundays were family days. No matter what we were doing in the morning, dinnertime was our time together as a family. I have to admit there were a few Sundays I had to spend either at work or in my home office doing some kind of paperwork. However, Sunday dinners always consisted of a home-cooked meal. So Sundays became the day I felt more oriented in the parental role of father and husband.

Cecelia always kept me focused and down to earth so that I could complete other life tasks and challenges in my career. We agreed when the children grew older, my parenting skills became essential in their maturation process. I apparently had better listening skills with young adults. I guess my listening and communication skills became handy when high school and college level issues became the dominant forces in our lives. Cecelia said I gave more logical advice with good sound reasoning needed by young adults. She was more available for emotional advice. Suddenly, there was a lot of respect for my expertise—finance.

Cecelia and I felt it was tough enough for children to find their own identities that there was no need to include them in my career rise. We always asked them if they would like to attend an event for my job. The majority of the time, they declined. So Cecelia had the job of attending events with me. I felt that to be successful in the corporate arena, the significant other needs to be that person's ears, heart and sounding board. Cecelia was that person to me.

Firstly, let me state that Cecelia loved meeting diverse people. It didn't matter what level of society a person came from. She was always herself. She was warm, friendly, sincere and honest—sometimes a little too honest but always with good intentions.

Secondly, I had a wife who loved to travel. So while I was working, she traveled the world, picking up information and art. She always found a place that became the focus of a conversation with someone new. It also helped that she loved to talk. Where I was quiet, Cecelia did the talking, sometimes peppered with humor but always interesting.

Thirdly, Cecelia didn't drink, and she found herself surrounded at times by people who sometimes let their behavior get out of hand by their drinking. She believed that type of behavior was not endearing and only made a person look silly. She believes bad actions will always be remembered because she is a black woman being checked out. Cecelia said games were always being played, and she understood that some situations needed a little game playing. She could play the games and still keep a sense of herself. While I did not agree, I felt there was no need for games—political or otherwise.

For example, Cecelia had heard about a certain partner who was not subtle about not supporting me. She made sure that every time she saw the partner in crowded public places she would give him a little peck on his cheek or make an elaborate statement about how great he looked. He would become very embarrassed by this. She knew this type of action would unnerve him and bring great satisfaction to her.

She said sometimes she didn't mind educating whites (who had never been around blacks) socially. As she got older, Cecelia realized that blacks were still being graded mostly on their race and not by who they are. Whites are still socializing primarily with their own kind. However, Cecelia acknowledges that whites' comfort level with people of color is a personal issue that will vary from person to person. But still, the majority of whites don't feel the need to socialize with colleagues of different races outside of work. This prevents the development of true interracial relationships. It is this non-workplace socialization that truly helps one gain a fuller understanding of the whole person, not just the person you see in the workplace.

Cecelia said the more things change, the more they stay the same. When I retired, she was just happy that we could travel more. We did agree that all aspects of our life together were managed by compromises

Those early life experiences taught me that no one achieves success alone, and we rarely see how much those small, mundane actions of caring can impact another until much later in our lives. We all have it in us to make a difference, but we have to get involved in life to do it.

Success is not only driven by hard work and skills, but also by giving back. Simple gestures such as tutoring kids who need reading or math; providing for the homeless and elderly; cleaning up and beautifying inner city parks; painting and repairing inner city schools; or mentoring high school students who were never told college was an option.

It's the giving back, the getting involved in life that provides me with my greatest satisfaction, and it's this kind of impact that cannot be measured by a financial statement or one's own net worth. When all is said and done, we'll be remembered by who we touched, what impact we've made on others' lives.

Of course this requires that one learn how to prioritize family and work while leaving enough time to give back. I always told any community organization that wanted me to volunteer that having time to spend with my family was important and after that I had to make sure I was successful at KPMG. The more successful I was at KPMG, the more I would be able to "give back."

I'm proud that during my tenure as chairman of the KPMG Foundation, I was able to lead the effort to make volunteering or "giving back" a core value of the firm. This was done through implementing what is now called INVOLVE, KPMG's national community involvement program. KPMG now has volunteer coordinators in each of the firms' more than 90 U.S. offices and provides employees 12 hours of paid volunteer time per year for work at any valid nonprofit organization. This program helps partners and employees actively support their communities through volunteerism.

Also, while on the foundation's board, I was instrumental in the implementation of the PhD project. This program, now approximately 12 years old, has as its foundation changing the ethnic mix of business school professors. The project helped increase the number of professors of color at numerous business schools from fewer than 300 to 700 in just one year. In addition, more than 400 people of color are enrolled in doctoral programs.

I'm proud of those services where I touched people and made a difference in their lives. I've served on the boards of universities, museums and major business groups, but working on the boards of small nonprofit organizations gave me the most satisfaction. Programs such as the Iona Senior Services project, a $1 million to $2 million organization, and Hoop Dreams Scholarship Fund, a $1.5 million organization, are examples of these types of organizations.

These organizations allowed me to use my business acumen to help people who are so focused with the day-to-day operation of the program that they often overlook the simple programmatic and governance needs. This is where I find my experiences and knowledge most helpful. I'm so gratified when I see how a program such as Hoop Dreams touches inner-city youth—changing their lives, giving them opportunities for college. While it's small and can't help many, it makes a world of difference in the lives of a few.

The Iona Senior Services program was introduced to me by Delano Lewis, a former president of NPR and later the ambassador to South Africa. The group actually wanted Del Lewis to become involved in its board, but because he was so busy, he asked me to get involved. I had no idea what a powerful impact this would make on my life.

Here was this small ecumenical organization serving Ward 3 in the District of Columbia. Its goal was to provide services to the elderly to keep them independent as long as possible. The clientele were mostly widows and women who had been professionals working in federal government all their careers and now were retired and mostly alone. Most had come to D.C. after World War II with their husbands and now were living alone.

I ended up joining the board of Iona Senior Services feeling uncomfortable around all these older—mostly white—women. There were only a few other blacks involved, but to their credit, they were making an effort to change that. They were grateful for my business background. And I was grateful to be doing something that would help me better understand what Cecelia was doing, as she was now a social worker specializing in the area of providing services to the elderly.

The group had a small office when I came aboard and was planning for a new building. I was elected president soon after joining the board and worked diligently to help the members realize their dreams. The city donated an old police station and its land to us for $1 a year for 99 years. I began leading the effort to solicit funding to help with our capital campaign, not knowing that Iona Senior Services' plans to build an office on the same street would incite a small war with the neighborhood association.

At the end of the first year, I was able to stabilize the fight while we continued to raise funds to lay the foundation for the building. The neighborhood group was convinced we'd never raise the funds; but we did, during the four years I was board president.

The Hoop Dreams Scholarship Fund was founded in 1996 by Susie Kay, who taught American government at H.D. Woodson High School in Washington for over a decade. Hoop Dreams began as a one-day event, a 3-on-3 charity basketball tournament staged to raise money for academic college scholarships for Kay's students. Since then, under Kay's leadership, a committed group of volunteers, supporters and a small staff have worked to grow the effort into a year-round not-for-profit organization. It is committed to expanding the academic and career horizons of D.C. public school students.

Since its inception, the Hoop Dreams Scholarship Fund has awarded more than 1,100 academic scholarships and helped send nearly 750 area high school students to college. More than 125 Hoop Dreams students have graduated from college, and many have returned to volunteer and mentor with the organization. Most of these graduates are the first in their family to go to college.

Volunteering gives me a balance and the satisfaction of giving back without expecting anything in return. When they close the book on our lives, few will remember us for what we had because we'll no longer have it, or by our lofty titles because the title will be transferred to the next in line. But we'll be remembered for the people we've touched and the differences we've made in their lives.

EPILOGUE

THE MEASURE OF A MAN

Sidney Poitier—one of America's great actors and the first male African American to win an Academy Award (for his role in "Lilies of the Field")—epitomizes success against the odds. While his is a different kind of success than mine, it's most certainly an all-American success story.

Poitier comes to mind because, like me, he's an American immigrant born in the Caribbean islands. In his second autobiography, *The Measure of a Man,* he shares an honest and introspective view of his 70-year journey, including 30-plus years of Hollywood stardom. But what he most poignantly shares is this truth: that achieving success is not the real measure of the man and not the most important part of the journey. The lessons learned during Poitier's journey from Cat Island in the Bahamas to Tinseltown and my own journey from St. Kitts in the West Indies to Yonkers, New York, are the real blessings of our journeys. How we share those blessings is the ultimate measurement.

Dr. Martin Luther King once said: "The ultimate measure of a man is not where he stands in moments of comfort and convenience, but where he stands at times of challenge and controversy."

I'm also reminded of something Sidney Poitier once said: "Don't settle for being as good; be better than. Raise the risk level."

Though our differences are so vast we could be from different planets, there are two things Sidney Poitier and I have in common: 1) We both had a strange accent when we set foot in this country; and 2) We both decided after growing older and wiser that there was something more than a long list of achievements and "firsts" we must leave behind.

In doing so, it's certainly my hope, and maybe his too, that others will find something of value—something more than the glitter and glamour from him or something more than old clients' profitability statements from me. Thus, following in that great actor's footsteps, I close this book with a few afterthoughts and suggestions for life.

What I have learned is that striving to be the best is an ongoing journey—one that requires continuous self-evaluation and a clear vision of where we are headed.

In business, as in our personal lives, success comes not only through hard work but also through recognition of new opportunities and the will to take advantage of these opportunities when they appear at your door.

Success requires that we ask the right questions about what the future holds. At the same time, we have to look back at where we've been, look at where we are today and visualize where it is we want to be in the future.

I'm convinced that the most important ingredient in achieving success is a strong value system. Whether we are conscious of it or not, our actions refer back to that value system instilled early in life. It directs our every move. I'm convinced, in these post-Enron years, that one of the key causes of the many failed businesses, jailed executives and lost investor dollars are the senior executives' value systems, or lack thereof.

We are all products of our early life—even senior executives of billion-dollar companies. The culture and heritage we derived from the country of our birth; the political and economic conditions that existed in the communities in which we were raised; our experiences during our formative years—early childhood, adolescence and teen years and even our early adulthood, college and early career years; out of all of this comes a value system that helps define who we are. It guides us as we tackle the problems we encounter in our personal and professional lives.

While I cannot claim perfection in either my personal or public life, I can claim that the value system instilled in me early in my life guided me and sustained me through some very rocky terrain. I can honestly say that seed planted so early bare fruit.

My very simple guidelines for success in life include:

- Prepare for tomorrow, not for today. Take a long view, not a narrow view. Always look to the future, learn from the past, but don't dwell on the past.

- Develop a strong work ethic. This means that you must study hard, work hard and always be prepared to take advantage of the opportunities that will come your way.

- Believe you can overcome all obstacles. Believe in yourself and practice focusing on the positive, never the negative. If you have self-respect and self-confidence, you will be successful.

- Remember that no one achieves success alone. For that reason, you must always reach out to others. Give back. Get involved in the world around you.

- Hold on to your core values and the knowledge that you are not here alone. Believe in a Supreme Being. There is a God. There is a Spirit. There is something that fuels you—a spirit that will guide you and develop you. During your life, you will be tested severely, but by falling back on your core values, you'll be served well.

- Cherish the moment! You will meet many people—some important, some ordinary. You will have many experiences, some more challenging than others. Take the time to learn as much as possible from all the people you meet and from all of life's experiences.

This simple value system—prepare for tomorrow, not just for today—guided me through my entire adult life and has helped me achieve any success that I have. That was the basis of my decision to go into accounting, realizing that it was a field that held many opportunities if I was given the chance to prove myself. I was convinced that I would be.

Planning and vision are what allowed me, approximately 10 years after joining the firm, to become Peat Marwick's first African-American partner. The first step is believing. After that comes the hard work.

In 1979, I transferred to the firm's Washington office. The move preceded a number of firsts for me at the company, including becoming partner in charge of the audit practice; managing partner of the Washington office; managing partner, Mid-Atlantic area; and being elected to the KPMG board of directors and subsequently the management committee.

Being the first, I always understood was a combination of good luck, good timing and working smart. The accolades didn't change who I was or what I was capable of doing. In fact, that told me more about the company and the people I worked with than about myself. What those firsts did, however, was reconfirm what I already knew—how important it is to be prepared to grasp opportunities when they come your way. Though none of us is certain when opportunities will appear, we have to live our lives in a way that we are always prepared to take advantage of them.

What young professionals should remember is that being the first meant that I was also confronted with many hardships and obstacles that those coming after me would not face. Without a doubt, racism was the most consistent, insistent obstacle during my journey toward success and one that is most difficult to confront. I always knew what my abilities were. I knew, in fact, that I was capable of much more than even my staunchest supporters conceded.

There's a really strange thing about the power of how others view you. Even I found myself sometimes questioning myself, when my abilities were constantly being questioned in oh-so-subtle and sometimes not-so-subtle ways by colleagues or managers. Was I "really" qualified for the position I was hired into? Was the job "given" to me because of quotas or affirmative action? Was I good enough, experienced enough for the role I sought? The game of corporate racism is almost always played as a mind game and can successfully erode the most capable person's sense of themselves if there isn't a strong foundation and self-confidence.

My brothers and I were raised as a family that didn't apologize for what or who we were. My Uncle Henry had more pride than anyone I've ever met, and he passed that on to us. He taught us that there was nothing we couldn't do as long as we knew we had to work harder at it. I remember how I used to sing "The Impossible Dream"—always confident that I would be successful.

Only with a strong value system to fall back on was I able to get through this with the attitude that I was capable and could overcome this and any other obstacle placed in my path. In short, I believed in myself and forced myself to focus on the positive aspects of each situation—ignoring, as much as possible, the negatives.

After some 40 years in the accounting profession, I have learned to keep in perspective what it means to be successful in your career and personal life—namely to do your best and try to find satisfaction in what you accomplish for the betterment of your family, the organization you work for, your profession, mankind and the fulfillment of your own life. I truly believe that my first step toward success was choosing the career that reflected what I truly believed in.

Finally, the greatest contribution any of us can make to mankind is to find a way to make a difference, to leave this world a better place than we found it. We do that by touching another human being in some significant way.

FRANK ROSS: THROUGH THE EYES OF THOSE WHO KNOW HIM

The following is a cross-section of interviews representing the men and women whose paths Frank Ross has crossed from a family member to friends and colleagues to his pastor. Each person offers poignant memories, anecdotes, personal assessments and projections for the legacy Frank Ross will leave. In short, they offer a measurement of the man, Frank Ross.

William R. Ross
(Frank's oldest brother)

"Frank was always very serious, more grounded. He was always told he would be a success at whatever he chose to be. No matter how much Frank accomplishes in his life, he never boasts about it or flaunts his success for others to see. He's a very modest person. He's always been a giver and has helped many, many people. He's generous with his time in the community, too. But, more than anything, Frank has always had ambitions to succeed, to do better."

———

Caspa Harris
(Former client, friend)

"From the beginning, I saw Frank as one of the finest individuals I'd ever met. He has 100 percent integrity. By far, Frank's greatest attribute was his understanding of accounting. That has served him well through-out his career.

"Personally, he was never an arrogant person, unlike many young professionals who felt they had to let everyone else know what they know. He got along with everyone; and when you brought a problem to him, he listened, looked at the whole picture and came back with his own version of whatever the subject was.

"Of course he had setbacks, but he never let them stand in his way of moving forward. He also was a beacon to many, many other minorities. What they saw was a person who didn't make it because of affirmative action, but because he did his job better than anyone else.

"You won't find a more devoted husband and father. He truly loves his wife; you can see it without him ever saying a word if you're ever around them. I truly admire that about him because when you've been around as long as I have, you've seen men destroy their homes and marriages during their most productive years. Frank was not like that at all."

Richard McKinless
(KPMG colleague)

"My wife, Kathy, and I credit Frank for our meeting and ultimately our marrying. We met because we were both assigned to the Howard University account under Frank. Kathy actually worked for Frank throughout her career at Peat Marwick, which later became KPMG. She made partner in 1986, two years before I did, then retired from KPMG in 2003. So, you could almost say that not only is he responsible for our careers, but also for our lives together. He certainly served as a mentor to both of us.

"I think one of the greatest lessons I learned from Frank was how to deal with clients and internal circumstances. Frank was the first mentor to tell me: 'You can only control certain things in your career, and everything else isn't worth losing sleep over. Most things you can't control, so learn to live with it or you'll end up trying to hold yourself to a standard you can't possibly achieve.'

"An awful lot of people of Frank's stature love to hear themselves talk. You would never say that about Frank Ross. When he chose to speak, you knew it was because he felt strongly about it.

"I think a big part of Frank's legacy will be the establishment of the National Association of Black Accountants. He was one of the founding board members and served as president. I think Frank's whole purpose in founding NABA was to establish a national networking vehicle for the few black professional accountants scattered throughout the country in various accounting firms.

"Other attributes that will also serve as part of Frank's legacy is his volunteerism. Once he was in a leadership position, he made sure we had policies in place at KPMG that encouraged volunteerism. Our office and the San Francisco office were the first to match employees' volunteer hours to charity.

"Frank saw that if you motivate young people to commit themselves to a volunteer effort, you will ultimately reap the benefits through higher productivity on the job.

"Because he is a man of few words, Frank practices what he preaches. I think part of his legacy is one of the unfinished works he's left for younger partners. He'd say, 'Yes, we've come a long way, but the journey is hardly over.'

"Frankly, there was a time when that was hard for Frank to voice if he perceived a lack of fairness. He picked his fights carefully. That meant he accepted a lot of things when he didn't want to. He knew that if he took on the fight and lost, he would have forfeited his ability to help in another way. He knew how to get things done."

Bennie Hadnott

(Friend)

"Frank's strength is that he's a very technical person. He has the ability to focus. He taught me the importance of focusing, staying attuned with what's happening around me.

"Frank was a high achiever. I'm not sure whether that is the result of a fear of failure, but whatever it was, it helped him succeed at KPMG. That Frank Ross fire and determination is what I saw when he convinced me to join the firm.

"NABA is the best thing Frank could possibly contribute to his legacy. The organization has made a huge difference in the accounting community. The effort has helped hundreds of people.

"Frank's other contribution is the Howard University Center for Accounting Education. He set the agenda and framed the curriculum for the future. He continues to be involved, working to help train young black students and professionals how to make it in the professional arena. As he moved up the corporate ladder, he never forgot his roots.

"One of the best lessons he taught me was the importance of taking risks. He told me: 'You're certain to fail if you try, but that shouldn't stop you.' "

Dan Robinson

(KPMG colleague)

"Frank has always been a wonderful person to be around. Bright, likeable, but yet not so soft he doesn't know how to get business done. We had a lot of fun together, and sometimes we had some pretty tense times.

"He earned the respect of his peers, not just his black colleagues. The very fact that he rose to the level he did is as much a tribute to him as anything. He wasn't brought in because he was black. He would not have risen to the height he did had he not had the abilities.

"Frank is someone young people can look up to. He works hard. He led the way for others to follow."

Ron McGowan
(KPMG colleague)

"When Frank came on board I could see right away that we are two completely different people. He's a lot more mild-mannered and plays the game a lot better. I was more of a hot head. Frank took care of things 'under the radar.' If you were a third party, you wouldn't know what he'd done. Frank also understands the environment and played within the rules.

"Frank Ross' legacy is that he allows young people to believe: 'You, too, can make it in the profession, through Peat Marwick, through NABA.' "

Theresa Hammond
(Author, "Blacks in Accounting")

"I personally found Frank Ross to be a very calm man and obviously very competent. He's quiet, but he's also very self-confident.

"He's a straight-forward person—says exactly what he means. I think the phenomenal thing is that as he has moved higher in his own career, he has continued to reach back and bring others with him. He has a very natural way of making young people believe that they can achieve, just as he did.

"Frank is such an accomplished person who is incredibly busy trying to do as much in the community and give back as much as he can. I always find it so wonderful that he gives credit to his aunt and uncle for raising him."

Susie Kay
(Community activist/colleague)

"When I met Frank, it wasn't long before I realized that he's truly a 'one in a billion' human being.

"He has truly been a pillar of strength for our Hoop Dreams academic project board. There are a lot of people out there who want to do the right thing, but not that many who know how to go about doing it. Frank does. He's very level-headed, focused and not much for talking and doing nothing. When I express my anxieties about the project all I have to do is have a conversation with Frank, and I'm ready to give it my best, again.

"Frank epitomizes everything we're trying to reinforce with Hoop Dreams. He is the inspiration these youth need to know they can achieve if they really want to.

"Frank Ross' legacy is how he lived his life. He said in his everyday actions: This is what it means to be a human being. He inspires others to be better human beings. Most importantly, I think, is that hundreds of young people are going in a much more positive direction thanks to Frank's leadership, his navigation of this project and definitely the dollars his company infused in the project's operation."

Angela Avant
(KPMG colleague)

"Throughout most of my career, Frank has been a constant thread and a guiding force in my career.

"All I can say about Frank Ross is that he doesn't make noise, he doesn't like noise; and over the years lots of people have depended on him for advice and counsel.

"Frank's success is based on his brilliant mind, first of all; but also his quest for excellence. He's thorough, focused, diligent, committed to getting it done, getting it done right and having it recognized.

"His commitment and dedication since I've known him has been to make organizations better serve people who don't have that natural edge. That's such a huge focus for him.

"Frank has this way of making everything look easy. The level of involvement and engagement are something to marvel at. He has always been dedicated, committed to anything he takes on.

"Frank Ross leaves a legacy of integrity, stewardship and a trusted adviser. In the D.C. community, all the organizations he has served on, he made better from a business perspective.

"He is, first and foremost, a family man and a spiritual human being. He treasures his family. Everyone I know wants to be like Frank. And the good thing is, he ain't finished yet—he continues to do great things."

Tom Williams
(KPMG colleague and friend)

"We worked together on the professional development project in New York. We would do these "show and tell" events for new recruits. We traveled to New Jersey and New York to speak to college students about how great the firm was. Frank was always so sincere about it. Frank had a calm and deliberate personality, while I was hot headed and spoke my mind. He'd always try to calm me down, to tell me not to be so outspoken.

"I've always had a lot of respect for Frank. His leadership style is very quiet, but very effective. He's somebody who's not afraid to ask you for whatever it is he needs, but he does it very quietly. He gives you the benefit of what you'll get out of the deal.

"Frank is a superb fundraiser. The thing that makes people support him is that he won't just ask you to help, he'll give a check and his time. He's always consistent, has always worked hard; just very quietly. I don't think I've ever seen Frank angry to a point of yelling. He's one of those quiet leaders."

Elaine Hart

(Former administrative assistant)

"Frank's management style was very to the letter; he was very fair. He's very particular about little things like how you dress. He always said that if you don't want to wear the suit, bring it in anyway. He's a stickler for being professional, but he's also a very fair manager and leader.

"I think the one thing I learned from him is that race should never be an excuse or a reason for us not doing our jobs; and whether we like it or not, we would always have to go one step beyond everyone else to prove ourselves.

"If racial issues came up during my tenure with him, he never let them become obvious. Even if he was given a job because he was black, he proved to them that he had the skills and abilities. He never let his color be an issue. I would see things sometimes and get upset, but he always told me to choose my battles, that most things weren't worth taking the risk.

"Frank always had an open door policy. He made time for 'the little people,' workers from all levels in the organization. Some people would come to his office complaining that they should probably look elsewhere for a job . . . then he would help them find another job outside KPMG.

"Frank Ross' greatest attribute was his fairness. But while he was fair, it was not smart to make him angry. If he didn't like something, he wouldn't come out and say it but would mention it in a subtle way. When he mentioned it, I knew it needed to be changed. I can only remember him getting really angry one time, and he never stayed mad long.

"He had a humility about him that people who didn't know him took as a weakness, which was a big mistake. He was honest and truthful, and you always knew where he was coming from. You didn't have to second-guess him. He didn't get into political games, just said what he meant.

"There were some people in the organization that he had to prove himself to. When he came in, those people liked him from the very beginning but didn't respect him as an accountant. It wasn't until they actually saw him at his work or running his audit committee meetings that they changed their minds. People from throughout the company started seeking him out for information. Even people from outside the office would call for his knowledge and expertise. The higher he went in the company, the more his colleagues realized he knew what he was doing.

"What people will always remember about Frank is how he always was concerned about others, how he actually put others first. I think that was because he had help in his early life; he always made a point of helping others up the corporate ladder.

"He made time to give back to the community. He taught at Howard University for more than 20 years without a paycheck, and it was rare that he would miss a day. He loved teaching the students there, and he still does. His main focus was trying to get them to understand that there is a future for them in accounting.

"One thing I know about Frank is that in spite of how dedicated he was to his job, his family came first. You could always tell when he was talking to his wife or one of his children, he went into husband or daddy mode. Then, once the call was over, he went back to the professional mode."

———◆———

Bill Morgan
(KPMG colleague)

"Frank was always a rock. It was great serving on the firm's board of directors with him. He was always well-thought-of by his colleagues. He was a strong man of few words.

"I think what most people admired most about him was his listening skills. He'd listen to your side of an issue without interjecting; go away and come back with his well-thought-out opinion. Nine times out of 10, you end up agreeing with him. Unlike a lot of people at his level, Frank wasn't one to talk just to hear himself talk. He was a doer.

"NABA symbolizes as well as anything the way Frank doesn't just complain about a problem but finds a way to resolve it. He didn't just talk about the need for more blacks to be brought into corporate accounting, he went about building an organization that prepared them, trained them and gave them mentors to help guide them in the right direction.

"I wasn't surprised at Frank's rise in the firm; I always knew he would be successful. He has all the traits of a great leader: honesty, integrity, thoughtfulness. There was, even when he was younger, a maturity about him; and you knew then that anything he decided to do would be done well.

"He has an amazing ability to deal with almost any type of person. I never in all my years of knowing Frank heard anything from him that was either derogatory or negative. He's such a natural leader.

"I can recall so many times, the board would be sitting around the table going through some deliberation about some concern; everyone would offer their two cents. And finally, after everyone else had spoken their minds, Frank would offer a very cogent overview of the discussion and then share his own views—which might include the best ideas from others, plus some new ideas of his own. No matter how many times he did that, it always surprised people because he was such a quiet person.

"He has always seemed able to balance his career, his family life and his community involvement. He has been the most consistent person I have ever known, for 38 years."

—◆—

Dave Fowler
(KPMG colleague)

"I probably can't say much more than what everyone else has told you about Frank. He's a very smart man, was very dedicated to the firm for more than 30 years and probably had the best people skills of anyone I ever worked with.

"He was able to do what was absolutely necessary in that field—get clients to be confident in your ability and your integrity. He was also very effective that way with his colleagues—his fellow partners and the professional staff.

"Frank was able to take people by surprise with his modest, unassuming personality. People mistakenly thought that meant he didn't have anything worth saying. When he had something to say, you'd know it, and it was always substantive. But he wasn't one to waste time tooting his own horn. He was never pushy or demanding—just steadfast and even aggressive in a quiet, subtle way.

"There's no question that as one of the firm's first professional-level African Americans, Frank had a tough row to hoe.

"But, Frank didn't just serve African Americans as clients. He was successful at crossing the racial lines very effectively, which we know is not always easy to do. Frank has never been the kind of guy who gave credence to race being either a detriment or an easy way to climb the ladder in his career.

"Frank Ross was a huge success in the heavily white environment that KPMG was, and he did it with style and class."

George Miles
(Friend)

"Frank will be remembered for his good work with NABA. Thirty years ago, it was a very small organization. Two years ago, their meeting was in Orlando, Florida, and I was blown away to see how much the organization has grown. It is wonderful to see all of these young professionals representing accounting firms all over the country. That is Frank's legacy that he can see now.

"It's folk like Frank who are leaving the accounting community, who are best able to share with young people what to expect and what to look out for. It was great to see that the group awarded Frank with a medal. It was great to see youth honoring their elders, recognizing their contributions.

"Frank Ross is not only a role model for other blacks but for so many other folks, too. I hope they'll acknowledge this. He's an exceptional leader who gets along with all folk. That's not an easy accomplishment.

"The Frank Ross story is a great story that should be out there for young blacks to read. Having someone like Frank Ross to have tested the waters for you is such a blessing."

Milford W. McGuirt
(KPMG colleague)

"I always saw Frank as a role model. He never let his ego get out of hand and always was down to earth, easy to talk to. I'm really grateful that he took the time to give some of us who came later guidance and advice. Frankly, that's the kind of legacy I'd like to leave when I retire.

"What makes Frank stand out is that he leads by example. I've never seen him speak loud or show any anger. He's balanced and always professional in his leadership style. Some people's egos manage them . . . not Frank's. He manages his ego.

"He's been a role model for both my professional career and my personal life."

Bernie Milano
(KPMG colleague)

"Frank was always a very bright person, extremely professional and respectful of others. He held very high standards for himself, so naturally he expected the same from others.

"I know for a fact that Frank was courageous. He never let the fact that he was the only black in the firm stop him from doing what he believed. His accounts were always some of the more profitable ones.

"Some people would prefer to steer clear of the whole subject of diversity, and Frank could have certainly done that, but he acted on the courage of his convictions.

"Much of Frank's legacy will be his leadership of the D.C. office. He has been a significant mentor to so many people in the firm and has been an infinite source of knowledge for the firm. I think all of corporate America continues to struggle with the issue of diversity. Frank isn't the kind of person to talk a problem to death; he finds a way to resolve it.

"He's done phenomenal things with Howard University, teaching there for more than 20 years and working with the PhD project to encourage more black students to go into business school."

Bonnie Cohen
(Former client and friend)

"Frank Ross is smart, honorable, thorough and an amazing listener. He never asks anyone to do anything he's not willing to do."

Jack Miller
(KPMG colleague)

"Frank was a low-key man, soft spoken and pretty much an introvert; but not in a negative way. What I came to learn about Frank was that he really doesn't say anything until he has something to contribute.

"I was one of the partners who talked to him about running for the board of directors. I was convinced he would be a great addition to the board, especially since we needed a not-for-profit presence on the board. I was on the nominating committee and became one of Frank's advocates.

"I had to brief the board chair on the nominations, and when I began pushing Frank, the chair wasn't too convinced. He said: 'But Frank never talks . . . . Do we need a member who doesn't talk?' I immediately chimed in, explaining that I knew Frank very well, and that, although he was low-key, he was one of those 'understated' people who actually had plenty to say when the need arose. Thankfully, the chair trusted my judgment, and Frank was elected to the board. I don't think the chair ever regretted that decision. Frank, if given the chance, would always prove that he was an outstanding contributor to the firm.

"Frank was never solely interested in filling quotas. He saw minorities as a class that should be systematically moved into the firm. By doing it in a more methodical way, he had to be able to work with the whole. He also saw the need to 'develop' young accountants and went about helping form an organization (NABA) to do that.

"While you'd never find him out there in the streets demanding things, he was inside the offices working to make sure women and minorities are given fair opportunities. Frank was consistent in pushing the same things other black advocates did, but from 'inside the system.'

"What many folk overlooked was that Frank's leadership in KPMG's public sector division was also spelled out in his success in bringing in more women to the firm than most divisions. I think he realized early on that the public sector work was attractive to women, especially the areas of social responsibility—housing, children, etc. Frank Ross was absolutely critical to great leadership in the D.C. office.

"Frank Ross' legacy would be that of a quiet leader. People who don't know him well saw him as quiet and reserved; but what many people don't know is how capable he is. He always knew what he wanted to accomplish and was able to get others to cash in, to advocate for it. And only when it was absolutely necessary did he go beyond that to being a harsher form of Frank Ross.

"What many folk also don't know is that Frank Ross has been involved in most of the significant issues at KPMG during his career. He was at the table during most of the important meetings. He was at the table a lot, and he was a great contribution to those meetings.

"What he did through his own career is prove that you don't always have to be a squeaky wheel to get things done . . . that quiet guys can do great things, too."

———————◆———————

The Rev. Dr. William M. White, Jr.
(Clinton A.M.E. Zion Church)
(Frank's former pastor)

"I served as Frank's pastor for 10 years. I first met him when he served as the chairperson of the Trustee Board of Clinton African Methodist Episcopal Zion Church. I was immediately impressed by Frank's business acumen and leadership style. However, I was most impressed by his love for Christ and his church.

"Frank has demonstrated stupendous commitment and dedication in his stewardship of Christ and Clinton Church. He continues to be a stalwart of Clinton Church and to provide outstanding leadership.

"I consider Frank a quiet giant in Christendom. He's not one to draw a lot of attention to himself, yet he gives himself fully to the ministry of the church. Many of his contributions of time, talent and resources go unknown, but God undoubtedly is pleased with his record of service. Frank is an excellent example of Christian discipleship."

The End

TO GOD BE THE GLORY!

REFERENCES/BIBLIOGRAPHY

The following documents, books and resources were used as research in writing this book:

"The History Makers," Frank K. Ross interview, April 25, 2001

The Star Spangled Hustle, Arthur I. Blaustein and Geoffrey Faux, Doubleday,

Journal of Accountancy, "Responsibility to Embrace Diversity," Bert N. Mitchell, October 2005

Knowledge@Wharton, online journal, (http://knowledge.wharton.upenn.edu)

Journal of Accountancy, "A History of Determination, Minority CPAs Have Come a Long Way, But True Diversity Has Yet to be Achieved," Phaedra Brotherton, October 2005

A White-Collar Profession: African American Certified Public Accountants Since 1921, Theresa Hammond, 2002

New Accountant, "Are Black Accountants Mainstreaming?" William Aiken, CPA, and Helen L. Brown, CPA, February 1989

"The National Association of Black Accountants (NABA), a Brief History," Helen G. Gabre, 2003

Design Almanac, "Ross Home Reflects the Free Spirit of its Owners," Robert Reed, August 31, 1988

Partners Memo newsletter, Peat Marwick Mitchell & Co., "Frank Ross Reports on Minority Employee Retention Project," November 13, 1978

Mid-Atlantic Area, Local News and Global Views, KMPM newsletter, "Meet Frank Ross," April 1996

Spectrum newsletter, National Association of Black Accountants, "Reflections on NABA's First Twenty Years and a Challenge for its Future," Frank K. Ross, Spring 1990

Washington Business Journal, Journal Profile: "Frank K. Ross, Giving Back is Fact of Life for New Peat Marwick Boss," Fred O. Williams, November 1996

Suburban People magazine, Reaching out, "Winston Ross: The Quiet Man, Westchester's NAACP Leader Speaks Softly and Accomplishes Much," Phil Waga, July 29, 1990

About the Author

Frank K. Ross is a visiting professor of accounting at Howard University. He is also director of Howard's School of Business Center for Accounting Education.

Mr. Ross retired from KPMG LLP in 2003 after more than 38 years of service. While at KPMG, he served as the Mid-Atlantic area managing partner for audit and risk advisory services and managing partner of the firm's Washington office. In addition, he was a member of KPMG's board of directors and chairman of the board of the KPMG Foundation.

In 1968, Mr. Ross was one of the nine co-founders of the National Association of Black Accountants. He served as the organization's first president.

Mr. Ross received a bachelor's degree in accounting and an MBA degree from Long Island University. In 1998, he received the Distinguished Alumni Award from LIU and an honorary doctorate of humane letters in 2001. He was the first graduate of the School of Business, Public Administration and Information Services to be honored by the university. In 2004, the University of the District of Columbia also awarded Mr. Ross an honorary doctorate of humane letters.

Mr. Ross is a member of the board of directors of the following corporations: Pepco Holdings Inc., Cohen & Steers Mutual Funds Group, and NCRIC Group Inc. In addition, he serves on the board of the following not-for-profit organizations: Gallaudet University, Hoop Dreams Scholarship Fund Inc., The Greater Washington Urban League, and the Howard University Chartered Middle School for Math and Science.